Essential SQA EXAM PRACTICE

HIGHER COMPUTING SCIENCE

Practice Questions & Exam Papers

QUESTIONS & PAPERS

Practise **25+ multi-part questions** covering every topic

Complete **2 practice papers** that mirror the real SQA exams

David Alford

HODDER GIBSON
AN HACHETTE UK COMPANY

Every effort has been made to trace all copyright holders, but if any have been inadvertently overlooked, the Publishers will be pleased to make the necessary arrangements at the first opportunity.

Although every effort has been made to ensure that website addresses are correct at time of going to press, Hodder Gibson cannot be held responsible for the content of any website mentioned in this book. It is sometimes possible to find a relocated web page by typing in the address of the home page for a website in the URL window of your browser.

Hachette UK's policy is to use papers that are natural, renewable and recyclable products and made from wood grown in well-managed forests and other controlled sources. The logging and manufacturing processes are expected to conform to the environmental regulations of the country of origin.

Orders: please contact Bookpoint Ltd, 130 Park Drive, Milton Park, Abingdon, Oxon OX14 4SE. Telephone: (44) 01235 827827. Fax: (44) 01235 400401. Email education@bookpoint.co.uk. Lines are open from 9 a.m. to 5 p.m., Monday to Friday, with a 24-hour message answering service. Visit our website at www.hoddereducation.co.uk. If you have queries or questions that aren't about an order you can contact us at hoddergibson@hodder.co.uk.

© David Alford 2019

First published in 2019 by
Hodder Gibson, an imprint of Hodder Education
An Hachette UK Company
211 St Vincent Street
Glasgow, G2 5QY

Impression number	5	4	3	2	1
Year	2023	2022	2021	2020	2019

Illustrations by Aptara Inc.

Typeset in India by Aptara Inc.

Printed and bound by CPI Group (UK) Ltd, Croydon CR0 4YY

A catalogue record for this title is available from the British Library.

ISBN: 978 1 5104 7176 4

SCOTLAND EXCEL
We are an approved supplier on the Scotland Excel framework.
Schools can find us on their procurement system as:
Hodder & Stoughton Limited t/a Hodder Gibson.

FSC
www.fsc.org

MIX
Paper from responsible sources
FSC™ C104740

CONTENTS

INTRODUCTION

Higher Computing Science

How to use this book

The purpose of this book is to provide you with focused exam practice. The first part of the book contains practice questions divided into the two question types that you will see in the question paper, together with advice on answering each type of question. The first part is split across the four areas of study: Software design and development, Computer systems, Database design and development and Web design and development. This part has a student margin stating the content being assessed in that question.

The second part of this book contains two complete question papers designed to mimic closely the question paper you will face. The book contains answers and also a Key Skills Grid that allows you to target your revision on a specific area of content should you require further practice on a specific topic.

This book can be used in two ways:

1   You can complete a practice question using your notes and books. Try the question first, and then refer to the answers to ensure you have sufficient detail to gain all the available marks. If you are unable to answer a question or discover your answer was not to the required standard you should refer to your notes and books. The practice questions are divided into areas of study so are ideal for doing this.

2   You can complete an entire practice paper under exam conditions, without reference to books or notes, and then mark your answers using the answers provided. This will give you a clear indication of the level at which you are currently working and enable you to target any areas of content in which you need to improve. The two complete papers in the second part of the book are ideal for doing this.

The course

Prerequisite knowledge

Before starting this course, it is expected that you will have passed National 5 Computing Science. The content of Higher Computing Science will build upon the skills and knowledge gained at National 5 level.

The Assignment

The Assignment will be worth 50 marks. This will be combined with a 110 mark question paper to give a total of 160 available marks.

The Assignment will have 25 marks assigned to Software design and development, 10–15 marks assigned to Database design and development and 10–15 marks assigned to Web design and development. The Assignment does not assess Computer systems and all assessment of this area of study will take place through the question paper.

The Assignment will require you to show your understanding and skills in the following areas:

▶   Analysis of a problem – 5 marks
▶   Design of a solution – 5 marks
▶   Implementation of a solution – 30 marks
▶   Testing a solution – 5 marks
▶   Evaluation of a solution – 5 marks

The question paper

The question paper will assess your problem-solving ability, making reference to technical knowledge on the areas stated within the Course Specification. The Course Specification document can be accessed from the Higher Computing Science section of the SQA website. This document has a number of appendices designed to clarify the content and it is advised that all candidates study these to ensure understanding of the key points that they cover.

Where questions involve a candidate interpreting program code, the code will be in SQA reference language. Candidates are not required to answer in SQA reference language, only to read and understand it. The full specification for SQA reference language can be accessed from the Higher Computing Science section of the SQA website, under Course Support, Reference language (www.sqa.org.uk/sqa/files_ccc/Reference-language-for-Computing-Science-Sep2016.pdf).

The current format of the question paper consists of 110 marks.

Section 1 will consist of individual problem-solving questions and is worth a total of 25 marks.

Section 2 will consist of longer, scenario-based problem-solving questions and is worth a total of 85 marks.

Hints and tips

Below is a list of hints and tips that will help you in your SQA exam paper:

▶ Make sure you read each question carefully. The detail in the question sets the scene for the problem to be solved.

▶ Refer to the situation described in the question. The papers are designed to test how a candidate applies their knowledge to a situation.

▶ Use technical terms. A Higher level answer will require certain terms from the course to be used.

▶ No marks will be given for repeating information given in the question. You can and should refer to the question, but build on that with the points you wish to make in order to gain the marks.

▶ Include as much detail as you can. As you will see from the answers in this book, many questions have multiple possible answers. If a marker deems that you lack enough technical detail to give you a mark on one point, they can still give you the mark for a separate, fully explained point. As much as possible, SQA markers undertake positive marking. This means that if a question is worth 2 marks, and a candidate makes one wrong point and two correct points, they will be awarded the 2 marks.

▶ When doing questions involving calculations, show all your working. If you make a small mistake under pressure, you will still gain some of the available marks.

▶ Ensure you have a scientific calculator with you in the exam.

▶ Attempt all questions. Leaving an answer blank means you will definitely receive no marks for it.

▶ Some candidates will have used programming languages where arrays are indexed beginning with element [1]. In SQA exams, arrays are indexed from 0, not 1.

▶ Access the Course Specification from the Higher Computing Science section of the SQA website to guide your revision.

Regular revision from the outset of the course is the best way to ensure you can recall the full detail required. Set aside time each week for this.

Remember, sometimes your biggest resource is people. Speak to your teacher about any concerns that you have, support your classmates and enjoy their support in return.

Good luck realising your potential in Higher Computing Science.

KEY AREA INDEX GRID

Key area	Practice Questions		Paper 1		Paper 2	
	Section 1	Section 2	Section 1	Section 2	Section 1	Section 2
Software design and development						
Development methodologies	2	1b, 2a	11	18a	2	
Analysis		1a, 1b, 3a, 3b	5			
Design		1c, 3c	21d			13e
Implementation (data types and structures)		1c, 1f	14a	15c, 15d	7	
Implementation (computational constructs)	1	1c, 1d, 1e, 1g, 2e	4, 13	14b, 15a, 15b, 21a, 21b	8	11e, 13a, 13d, 13f, 15a
Implementation (algorithm specification)	3	1f		18c, 19a, 21d		11a, 11d
Testing		2c, 3d, 3e		15e, 18b		11b, 11c, 13b, 13c, 15b
Evaluation		2b, 2d, 2f				
Computer systems						
Data representation	1		1, 2, 3	20d, 21c	1, 3	14b, 14c
Computer structure	2	1b, 1c, 1d	9		4	16b
Environmental impact	3	1a		17d		
Security risks and precautions	4, 5, 6	1e, 1f	10	19b, 19c		
Database design and development						
Analysis	4	1a				
Design	1, 3	1b, 1c, 2a, 2b, 2e	6, 7	16a, 16b, 22a		12a, 12b, 16a
Implementation	2	1d, 2b, 2c, 2f, 2g		16c, 22b, 22c, 22d		16c, 16d
Testing				16d	5	
Evaluation		2d			5	
Web design and development						
Analysis						17a
Design	3	1a	12a	17c, 20a		17b
Implementation (CSS)	5	1b, 1c, 1d, 1e, 1f, 1g, 2a, 2c		20b, 20c	6	17c
Implementation (HTML)	1	1b, 1g	12b	17a, 17b	9	17d
Implementation (JavaScript)	2	2b, 2d			10	12c
Testing	4	2e	8	15f		14a
Evaluation		1h				17e
Total Marks	/34	/110	/25	/85	/25	/85

Section 1 questions

>> HOW TO ANSWER

Section 1 in the question paper will consist of several short problem-solving questions worth 1–4 marks. They may be split into two or three parts. Each question will relate to one of the four areas of study, i.e. Software design and development, Computer systems, Database design and development or Web design and development. Often there is information given in the question about a scenario or situation. You should refer to that situation in your answer.

Questions are likely to be of 'C' or 'B' level of difficulty. Be sure to use the computing terminology that you learned in your Higher course in your answers.

Top Tip!

Look for the command words: if a question says 'explain' or 'describe' then you must be sure to include technical detail justifying your answer. If a question says 'state', a shorter answer is often sufficient, but there is no harm in including extra detail if you know it.

	MARKS	STUDENT MARGIN

Software design and development

Questions set within a scenario, assessing content from the Software design and development area of study. Each worth between 1 and 4 marks.

1 Joyce's program has an integer variable called `result` that holds the number of seconds she took to finish a triathlon. She knows there are 60 seconds in a minute. She would like two variables, one holding the number of minutes and the other the remaining number of seconds to be used to output data. For example, if the result was 607 the output of her program would read 'You took 10 minutes 7 seconds'.

Program code:

```
DECLARE result, s, m AS INTEGER
INITIALLY 0
RECEIVE result FROM KEYBOARD
m=INT(result/60)
s=_____
SEND "You took " & m & " minutes "
& s & "seconds" TO DISPLAY
```

Implementation (computational constructs)

Top Tip!

There are four types of pre-defined functions that you need to be able to code:
- substring
- conversion between a character and its ASCII value
- changing a real number to an integer
- modulus.

a) Using a programming language of your choice to implement modulus, complete the missing line above to calculate the contents of the variables. **1**

b) Explain why the pre-defined function INT() has been used in the above code. **1**

2 Explain why it is less likely that, after the initial release of a program, a new feature will be added via an update if a program has been developed using an agile methodology rather than an iterative one. **2**

Development methodologies

Hint!

When comparing two methodologies, be sure to mention both in your answer.

	MARKS	STUDENT MARGIN

3 Briony works for a delivery company. She has written an algorithm that will search for a target ID code from a list of 18 parcels. Each parcel has a unique parcel ID code, stored in the array named `parcel_code[]`. Part of the algorithm is shown below.

```
DECLARE found INITIALLY false
RECEIVE target_code FROM
KEYBOARD
FOR iteration = 0 TO 17 DO

_____

  SET found TO true
  END IF
END FOR
```

What command is missing in line 4?

MARKS: 1

STUDENT MARGIN: Implementation (algorithm specification)

> **Top Tip!**
> There are four standard algorithms that you should be able to recognise and code:
> * find the maximum
> * find the minimum
> * linear search
> * count occurrences.
> They may be adapted to suit specific problems and might take careful inspection of the code to identify them.

Computer systems

Questions set within a scenario, assessing content from the Computer systems area of study. Each worth between 1 and 4 marks.

1 State the range of denary integers that can be stored if 11 bits are used to represent positive and negative integers using two's complement.

MARKS: 2

STUDENT MARGIN: Data representation

> **Top Tip!**
> In two's complement there is not a bit for the sign (like you see in floating point conversion as part of the mantissa).

> **Hint!**
> Remember that one of the possible unique binary codes is for zero.

2 Jerome sees an advert for two newly released computers. The advert states that one has a higher clock speed.

a) Explain why a higher clock speed might result in greater computer performance.

MARKS: 1

b) Describe a situation where a higher clock speed would not improve computer performance.

MARKS: 1

STUDENT MARGIN: Computer structure

> **Top Tip!**
> There are four factors affecting computer performance that you should be able to explain in detail:
> * the number of cores
> * the number of lines on the data bus
> * the cache
> * the clock speed.

	MARKS	STUDENT MARGIN

3 Studies have shown that more harmful gases are emitted by cars in a journey where they have to slow down then accelerate. Harmby Council have decided to install an intelligent system with vehicle detectors to monitor road traffic approaching a busy junction and thereby decrease instances of traffic being stopped at traffic lights. Describe how this intelligent system could help the environment.

MARKS: 1 — STUDENT MARGIN: Environmental impact

Top Tip! For questions asking about intelligent systems it is recommended that you mention the system taking action based on what it has learned from past experience or trends. Some systems that take action based on input from sensors are not actually always deemed intelligent (e.g. thermostatic heating).

4 Celine was curious about the security measures in place at the clothing chain that she works for. At home on her day off she uses her own computer to attempt to hack into the company's server but is unsuccessful.

Describe any implications for her as a result of the Computer Misuse Act 1990. Justify your answer.

MARKS: 2 — STUDENT MARGIN: Security risks and precautions

Top Tip! The Computer Misuse Act 1990 is the only law you could be specifically asked about at Higher level. It contains three distinct offences.

5 A prominent social network was recently the victim of a Denial of Service attack. Explain two reasons why an individual or group might have decided to undertake such an attack.

MARKS: 2 — STUDENT MARGIN: Security risks and precautions

6 Frode has encrypted a digitally signed document with the receiver's public key and sent it across the internet to the receiver.

a) Describe how this document will be decrypted by the receiver.

MARKS: 1

b) Explain why Frode has digitally signed the document.

MARKS: 1

STUDENT MARGIN: Security risks and precautions

Hint! When a digital signature is used, it is generated by using both the sender's private key and the content of the message. It is verified at the receiving end using the digital signature, the public key and the message.

MARKS | STUDENT MARGIN

Database design and development

Questions set within a scenario, assessing content from the Database design and development area of study. Each worth between 1 and 4 marks.

1 A DIY store has three separate departments. Each department has its own manager. A manager will only manage one department. Each department has two or more employees. An employee will only work for one department. Complete the entity-occurrence diagram below to show this.

2 | Design

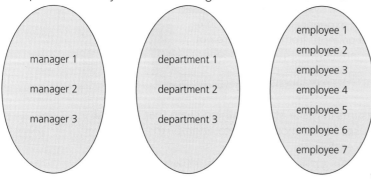

> **Top Tip!** An entity-occurrence diagram shows the state of the records in a database at one particular point in time, specifically their relationships with other records.

> **Hint!**
> There are a few correct answers here as the detail given in the question relates to tables rather than individual records.

2 A database table is shown below.

3 | Implementation

Table: Product			
type	**productID**	**productName**	**stockLeft**
print	p12	black ink	12
office	o31	staples 8mm	9
print	p94	white A4 paper	40
office	o82	blue pens	26
office	o22	paper clips	11

Show the output from the following SQL statement:

```
SELECT type, MIN(stockLeft) AS [Lowest stock level] FROM
Product GROUP BY type;
```

> **Hint!**
> In a question where you must interpret SQL, the first thing to look for is *GROUP BY* as this indicates how many rows to show in your answer. This SQL statement also features an alias and an aggregate function.

	MARKS	STUDENT MARGIN
	2	Design

3 Landon works in the office at West Ayrshire Council. The council keep track of employees in a database which has the following two tables:

Occupation	Site
<u>Job Title</u>	Site Name
Wage	<u>Telephone Number</u>
	Address

An employee's job title can be one of 'Teacher', 'Office', 'Janitor', 'Kitchen', 'Classroom Assistant' or 'Cleaner'.

Landon plans to add a third table called 'Employee' to the database, to keep track of each individual staff member. Landon plans to use a compound key for this new table. Explain what a compound key is and why this might lead to problems in this situation.

> *Hint!*
>
> Where answers include explaining what a compound key is, SQA are looking for a lot of detail so be sure to explain as fully as you can.

4 Frankton High School has held elections for student council representatives every year for the past 30 years. Each candidate in an election had a unique number and they each received a number of votes. The council was made up of the two students from each year group who gained the most votes.

A database is required to store data on the council for each year, the elections and the candidates. Users should be able to find how many votes a candidate got or see the student council members for any given year.

State two functional requirements of the database.

Marks: 2 — Analysis

> *Hint!*
>
> Be sure to keep in mind that functional requirements must be worded differently from user requirements. Any sentence beginning, 'Users must be able to…' or similar is not stating a functional requirement.

Web design and development

Questions set within a scenario, assessing content from the Web design and development area of study. Each worth between 1 and 4 marks.

1   Part of a web page contains an HTML form which will be used to survey which games consoles users own. This part of the HTML code is shown below.

```
<form>
<input type="radio" name="console" value="PB"> PlayBox <br>
<input type="radio" name="console" value="ZS"> Z-Station <br>
<input type="radio" name="console" value="BM"> Button Masher
</form>
```

a)   Show how you would expect the result of this HTML code to be displayed within a browser.

b)   Show how to add a button to the form containing the text 'OK'. When the button is clicked the form data should be submitted.

> **Top Tip!**   You need to know about five possible input types for HTML forms:
> - text
> - number
> - text area
> - radio
> - submit button.
>
> In addition, you should be able to recognise and implement the use of the `select form` element and the `id` attribute.

2   Jahnvi has created some HTML code containing JavaScript:

```
<p style="background-color:red;"
onmouseout="changeBG(this)">
Testing
</p>
```

Write the function that will change the background colour of the paragraph to yellow when the pointer leaves the paragraph.

> **Hint!**
> The JavaScript function has been named in the question so be sure to use this name. The use of 'this' shows that the paragraph has been passed in as a parameter: you can use any name other than 'this' for the formal parameter in your function.

MARKS

1

1

2

STUDENT MARGIN

Implementation (HTML)

Implementation (JavaScript)

	MARKS	STUDENT MARGIN

3 Dean is designing a website for his online printing business. The website will have a multilevel structure: there will be the home page with links to three main web pages – T-shirts, Mugs and Publications. The Publications web pages will have links to four sub-pages about Flyers, Posters, Magazines and Newsletters.

Design a multilevel structure for the site.

2   Design

4 PizzaDelite are creating a new version of their website that is designed to make it easy to order food on mobile devices. Describe two different personas that they might consider during usability testing.

2   Testing

> **Hint!**
> Give as much detail as you can to be sure of gaining the available marks.

5 Shauna has used JavaScript and CSS on a paragraph as shown:

```
<p onclick=this.style.
display="none">

By continuing to use this site
you accept our cookie policy.

</p>
```

Explain what happens to the paragraph when it is clicked.

Top Tip!

There are three values for the CSS display property that you must be familiar with:
- block
- inline
- none.

1   Implementation (CSS)

Section 2 questions

| | MARKS | STUDENT MARGIN |

Software design and development

Longer questions with many parts, each part of a question is set within the same scenario. These assess content from the Software design and development area of study.

1   Simeon is following an iterative development process in creating a program to analyse levels of carbon dioxide in the Earth's atmosphere. The unit of measurement for this is called ppm (parts per million). It will process the measurements for the past 40 years, one measurement per year.

   a)   Identify the boundaries of this proposed software.

   MARKS: 2 — STUDENT MARGIN: Analysis

   ### Hint!
   Include any boundaries that you can see in the situation given, to be sure of gaining all available marks.

   b)   Explain why an accurate statement of the purpose, scope, boundaries and functional requirements is vital at the analysis stage of an iterative development process.

   MARKS: 2 — STUDENT MARGIN: Analysis

   ### Hint!
   The iterative development process has six stages. The key here is to think about how the results of the analysis stage are used at each of the following stages.

   c)   The 40 years and the measurements are stored in a CSV file. Part of the file looks like this:
   … 1996,362.58,1997,363.48,1998, 366.27 …
   Show using a structure diagram how this data could be read from the file into two parallel one-dimensional arrays.

   MARKS: 5 — STUDENT MARGIN: Design Implementation (data types and structures) / Implementation (computational constructs)

   ### Top Tip!
   You will often see problem-solving questions that combine different concepts from within the area of study. Here you are being assessed on structure diagrams, data flow, file handling and parallel one-dimensional arrays.

	MARKS	STUDENT MARGIN

d) At the implementation stage the data is in two arrays called `year[]` and `reading[]`. Simeon has taken an existing function that calculates an average and amended it. The code is shown below:

```
FUNCTION findAve (ARRAY OF REAL list) RETURNS REAL
   DECLARE total, average AS REAL INITIALLY 0.0
   FOR index FROM 0 TO 39 DO
      SET total TO total+list(index)
   END FOR
   SET average TO total/40
   RETURN average
END FUNCTION
```

State the scope of the total variable.

MARKS: 1

STUDENT MARGIN: Implementation (computational constructs)

> **Hint!**
> When asked to state the scope of a variable there are two possible answers: 'local' or 'global'.

e) Simeon's program contains this subprogram:

```
PROCEDURE showAve (ARRAY OF REAL reading)
   DECLARE aveReading AS REAL INITIALLY 0.0
   findAve(reading, aveReading)
   SEND "Average CO2 level: " & aveReading TO DISPLAY
END PROCEDURE
```

Explain why line 3 of the procedure above will result in an error; show the correct line of code.

MARKS: 2

STUDENT MARGIN: Implementation (computational constructs)

> **Top Tip!** You should know the differences in how each of the two kinds of subprogram are used.

f) Using a programming language of your choice, implement the algorithm to display the year with the highest carbon dioxide measurement and the reading for that year. Your answer should use the arrays `year[]` and `reading[]`.

MARKS: 5

STUDENT MARGIN: Implementation (algorithm specification)

Implementation (data types and structures)

> **Top Tip!**
> There are four standard algorithms that you should be able to recognise and code:
> • find the maximum
> • find the minimum
> • linear search
> • count occurrences.

> **Hint!**
> Here you have to combine one of the standard algorithms with the implementation of two parallel one-dimensional arrays.

		MARKS	STUDENT MARGIN

g) One team has written part of the program containing a menu of four choices. They have allowed the user to input a, b, c or d to make a choice and stored this in a variable called `choice`.

Another team is trying to process the `choice` variable in a different part of their program but has written code to deal with a choice of A, B, C or D.

Write the code that will convert the choice to its ASCII value, subtract 32, then convert back to the character again.

The result of this will be to change the lower case letter to upper case (the ASCII code for 'a' is 97, the ASCII code for 'A' is 65).

3 — Implementation (computational constructs)

Top Tip!

There are four types of pre-defined functions that you need to be able to code:
- substring
- conversion between a character and its ASCII value
- changing a real number to an integer
- modulus.

2 Adnan is working for a company producing a program to enable the operation of tills in a shop. This program is being developed by following an agile design methodology.

a) Compare an iterative design methodology with an agile design methodology in terms of teamwork.

2 — Development methodologies

b) One of Adnan's colleagues tells him that modular code has better maintainability.

Explain what makes code modular.

1 — Evaluation

c) Users of the program will have to log in with a username and password. The program will store the time of each of the last 100 successful logins by any user, and the username of whoever logged in at that time, in two parallel one-dimensional arrays called `login_time[]` and `username[]`.

Adnan has designed a feature to find all the logins by a given user:

1 — Testing

```
DECLARE target_user AS STRING
DECLARE found AS ARRAY OF BOOLEAN
RECEIVE target_user FROM KEYBOARD
FOR index FROM 0 TO 99 DO
   IF target_user=username[index] THEN
     SET found[index] TO true
   END IF
END FOR
FOR i FROM 0 TO 99 DO
   IF found[i] THEN
     SEND username[i] & login_time[i] TO DISPLAY
   END IF
END FOR
```

Before coding the above design, Adnan works through his design line by line with a set of test data using paper and pencil to track inputs, changes to variables and outputs. State the name given to this technique.

	MARKS	STUDENT MARGIN

d) Evaluate Adnan's design in part **c)** in terms of fitness for purpose and efficient use of coding constructs.

MARKS: 4 — *STUDENT MARGIN:* Evaluation

> **Top Tip!**
> - When evaluating fitness for purpose, you need to compare the statement of the problem with the solution. Here the statement of the problem is given at the beginning of part **c)**.
> - When evaluating efficient use of coding constructs, look to see if the code has any unnecessary variables, loops, conditional statements or other unneeded lines of code.

e) The shop employs 35 staff. The system assigns a username to employees by using the first four letters of their last name (surname) concatenated with the first three letters of their first name (forename). These are stored in arrays called `surname[]` and `forename[]`.

Using a programming language of your choice, write code to generate the usernames for the 35 employees of the shop, placing these in an array called `username[]`.

MARKS: 3 — *STUDENT MARGIN:* Implementation (computational constructs)

> **Hint!**
> This question is assessing your ability to implement parallel arrays, substring and concatenation. Be sure to use the array names given in the question.

f) The final program is evaluated in terms of robustness. Explain what is meant by robustness of a program and suggest one way that robustness can be ensured.

MARKS: 2 — *STUDENT MARGIN:* Evaluation

3 Morven works for a company that creates programs for architects and interior designers to use to create plans. Many of the objects in these designs are rectangular when displayed on a plan. Morven has been asked to develop a program to take in the name, length and breadth of a rectangular object from the keyboard, calculate the area and then display a scale graphic of the rectangle on screen with a message stating the object name, length, breadth and area.

a) State the purpose of this program.

MARKS: 4 — *STUDENT MARGIN:* Analysis

b) Suggest three deliverables within the scope of this program.

MARKS: 3 — *STUDENT MARGIN:* Analysis

> **Top Tip!**
> The term scope has a different meaning when used in or referring to the analysis stage than it does when used in or referring to the scope of a variable within the code.

c) Morven has decided to call the variables name, length, breadth and area. Morven has planned the following main steps:

1. Get inputs from user.
2. Calculate area.
3. Show rectangle graphic.
4. Show text outputs.

Indicate the data flow for these steps.

MARKS: 4 — *STUDENT MARGIN:* Design

> **Top Tip!**
> Remember, if a variable is not required for a step, then it doesn't flow in or out of that step.

	MARKS	STUDENT MARGIN

d) The value of the area calculated by the program is incorrect. Morven sets a breakpoint at the end of the code for step 2 of the design in part **c)**. Explain how a breakpoint could help Morven. — **2** — Testing

e) Suggest a more appropriate debugging technique for Morven to use and justify your choice. — **2** — Testing

Computer systems

In the exam, Section 2 questions are not set wholly on Computer systems but may have one or two parts addressing this area of study.

1 Bernard is designing a new embedded computer system to run inside a new model of petrol-powered car that is being developed. The system will take input from multiple sensors as well as from user actions and be responsible for a number of functions including climate control, anti-lock braking system, fuel injection, engine air flow, satellite navigation and in-car audio. The climate control takes into account past user decisions on temperature settings as well as data from a temperature sensor outside the car.

a) Give an example of one feature of the system that may indicate that it is an intelligent system. — **1** — Environmental impact

b) Explain how Bernard could include hardware to ensure sufficient computer system performance in this situation. — **2** — Computer structure

> **Hint!**
> Read the situation carefully to see if any requirements of the system stand out to you.

c) Bernard has designed a microprocessor that fetches instructions from main memory and executes them in sequence. Explain the steps involved in the fetch–execute cycle. — **3** — Computer structure

d) The microprocessor has a higher clock speed than the microprocessor in an older model of car from the same car manufacturer. Why does a higher clock speed improve system performance? — **1** — Computer structure

e) The system has both Bluetooth, to connect to audio devices, and Wi-Fi, to enable software updates to be downloaded when securely connected to the internet via the owner's home Wi-Fi network. Explain how this might lead to individuals attempting to break the Computer Misuse Act 1990. — **2** — Security risks and precautions

> **Top Tip!**
> The Computer Misuse Act 1990 is the only law in the Higher course, and it outlines three distinct offences.

f) The car company's website has been affected by a Denial of Service (DoS) attack. Describe one cost to a company that has been affected by a DoS attack. — **1** — Security risks and precautions

Database design and development

Longer questions with many parts, each part of a question is set within the same scenario. These assess content from the Database design and development area of study.

1   A local council employs several landscape operatives to use ride-on lawnmowers to maintain public areas of grass. They keep track of the data on this using a database:

Operative	Employee ID	PK
	Forename	
	Surname	

Mower	Registration	PK
	Make	
	Model	

Site	Site ID	PK
	Postcode	
	Description	
	Area in m^2	

The council wish a fourth table to be added to keep track of each individual visit to a site. They want to store which operatives went to the site and which mower they took. They want to be able to access the date of the visit, the time work was started and the time work ended. The council would like to be able to find the details of a visit quickly, whether they search by date of visit, operative or site. It is expected that multiple operatives on multiple mowers might be involved in a single visit.

a)   The council have stated a number of end-user requirements. Explain what is meant by end-user requirements.

b)   The Operative, Mower and Site tables shown above are not currently linked by a relationship. Explain why that is known from the information given above.

c)   Suggest suitable validation for the Area in m^2 field in the Site table.

d)   Write the SQL statement to show the total area in m^2 of all the sites in the council's database. Use an alias to name the result 'Total Area'.

Top Tip!
There are four types of database validation that you should know about.

Top Tip!
Examiners can be lenient on the correct use of brackets, speech marks or semicolons; however be sure to use the correct words in the correct place.

1   Analysis

1   Design

2   Design

3   Implementation

2   Jordan runs a company called Wholesale Grocers that supplies chopped, packaged and/or processed vegetable products to the catering trade. They source each vegetable from a specific farm. They keep track of the business in a database:

Farm		
Contact	Name	Contact Tel
Karen James	Waghill	555 7221
Lesley Waters	Hotglen	555 7890
David Rankin	Tamly	555 4122
Reuben Schultz	Canwick	555 3212
Hayden Kipekwa	Salworth	555 9876
Alice Hurt	Tiston	555 5611
Karen Plant	Longbay	555 6932

Ingredient			
Name	Bought for	Farm name*	Sold for
Carrot	0.05	Waghill	0.09
Cabbage	0.22	Hotglen	0.32
Corn	0.14	Tamly	0.23
Pea	0.02	Canwick	0.03
Green Bean	0.02	Salworth	0.05
Strawberry	0.20	Tiston	0.32
Raspberry	0.17	Longbay	0.30
Broccoli	0.24	Waghill	0.32
Cauliflower	0.24	Hotglen	0.35
Turnip	0.23	Tamly	0.31
Potato	0.12	Canwick	0.17
Onion	0.09	Salworth	0.16
Garlic	0.03	Tiston	0.10
Tomato	0.08	Longbay	0.20

Order Line			
Order ID	Ingredient name*	Placed by*	Quantity
001	Raspberry	02	150
002	Broccoli	04	58
003	Cauliflower	01	60
004	Turnip	02	47
005	Raspberry	01	140
006	Strawberry	03	162
007	Raspberry	03	100
008	Broccoli	02	38
009	Cauliflower	04	60
010	Turnip	01	20
011	Potato	02	300
012	Onion	02	90

Caterer	
Company ID	Name
01	Luciano's
02	Tamly Hotel
03	Kit's Kitchen
04	Bistro Corner

a) Show the entity-relationship diagram for this database. On this occasion there is no need to include the attributes. Include the entity names and cardinality.

3   Design

> **Hint!**
>
> Remember, where you see a foreign key, that table is on the 'many' side of a relationship with the table for which that field is the primary key.

		MARKS	STUDENT MARGIN

b) All ingredients from Tiston farm are to have the amount they are bought for increased by 0.01. Write the SQL statement to do this.

c) Jordan has noticed that there is not a lot of profit to be made from peas.

They have written the following SQL statement:

```
DELETE Pea FROM Ingredient;
```

Explain the effect of this SQL statement.

> **Hint!**
> Note the command word 'Explain' in the question, indicating that you must give a detailed answer.

d) Jordan wants to see the names of the ingredients for whom David Rankin is the contact.

They plan to run the SQL query:

```
SELECT Farm.Contact, Ingredient.Name FROM Ingredient,
Farm WHERE Farm.Contact="David Rankin" AND Farm.Name =
Ingredient.[Farm Name] ORDER BY Ingredient.Name;
```

They hope for this result:

Contact	Name
David Rankin	Corn
David Rankin	Turnip

Evaluate the accuracy of output of the SQL statement.

e) Jordan has asked you to plan a query to show the number of order lines currently in the system for each separate ingredient. Complete the design below for this query:

Field(s) and calculation(s)	
Table(s) and query	
Search criteria	
Grouping	
Sort order	

> **Hint!**
> When planning a query, you should always be given the table as shown in this question. This does not mean all rows in the table have to be filled in. The number of marks assigned to the question is often an indicator of the number of distinct parts required in your answer – but not always. Also, two of these distinct parts of the answer might appear in the same row of the table.

f) Jordan plans to begin working with Sudbury farm after calling 555 6777 to speak to the contact there, called Jiri Plasil.

Show the correct SQL statement to add this new farm to the database.

g) Show the output from the following SQL statement:

```
SELECT [Ingredient name], Quantity FROM [Order Line] WHERE
[Ingredient name] LIKE "%berry" ORDER BY Quantity DESC;
```

3

Implementation

Top Tip! One popular database package uses the '*' character as its wildcard character, but it is more common to use '%'.

Web design and development

Longer questions with many parts, each part of a question is set within the same scenario. These assess content from the Web design and development area of study.

1 Zetsas Instruments is a company that sells musical instruments. They have developed a multilevel website to allow customers to browse and buy products. Part of the HTML for the home page is shown below:

```
…
<body>
<header>
<img src="banner1.jpg"> <br>
<nav>
<a href="p1.html">Brass</a> ~
<a href="p1.html">Woodwind</a> ~
<a href="p1.html">String</a> ~
<a href="p1.html">Percussion</a>
</nav>
</header>
<main>
<img src="shop.jpg">
<h3>About Us</h3>
<p class="intro">Zetsas Instruments is a family run
business that sell musical instruments through our shops
and our websites. Have a look or contact us if you have any
questions</p>
<img src="collection.png">
</main>
<footer>
<a href="mailto:zetsas@supramail.com"> Contact Us </a>
</footer>
</body>
</html>
```

a) Draw a wireframe that may have been used to design the layout of the home page.

3

Design

Top Tip! Remember, the actual text content of paragraphs for a web page does not appear on a wireframe design.

MARKS | STUDENT MARGIN

b) The owner of the company wants the images in the main area to be shown at a size of 250 × 250, without affecting the images in any other part of the page (such as the banner).

Show a CSS rule using descendant selectors that would do this.

> **Hint!**
>
> It would be easy to accidentally answer with a grouping selector instead of a descendant selector here as there is one small but important difference in the syntax between the two.

2 — Implementation (CSS), Implementation (HTML)

c) Show a CSS rule to change the text colour to red if the mouse pointer moves over the navigation bar.

2 — Implementation (CSS)

Top Tip!

There are three types of CSS with regard to where the rules are placed:

- external
- internal
- inline.

d) If using internal CSS, where would CSS rules be placed?

2 — Implementation (CSS)

e) The owner has added a new paragraph to the home page inside the first paragraph so that the HTML for the main area reads:

1 — Implementation (CSS)

```
...
<main>
<img src="shop.jpg">
<h3>About Us</h3>
<p class ="intro">Zetsas Instruments is a family run
business that sell musical instruments through our shops
and our websites. <p class="sale">Selected instruments
are on special offer!</p>
Have a look or contact us if you have any questions</p>
<img src="collection.png">
</main>
...
```

The owner has also added the following CSS rule:

```
.sale {display: inline;}
```

Explain the effect of the CSS rule on the newly added paragraph.

f) What would be the effect if the rule in part **e)** were then changed to the following?

```
.sale {display:block;}
```

1 — Implementation (CSS), Implementation (CSS)

g) Use a grouping selector to set the top and bottom margins of the header, main and footer areas to eight pixels.

2 — Implementation (HTML)

h) The owner doesn't want any padding around the introduction paragraph. State one advantage of having padding around a paragraph.

1 — Implementation (CSS), Evaluation

		MARKS	STUDENT MARGIN

2 Cressida Snacks sell flavoured oven-baked snack foods.

Currently part of their website's home page looks like this:

CS Cressida Snacks provide quality tasty snacks across the country. We have a range of products and flavours which are low in sugar. Ingredients are responsibly sourced and extensive use of local suppliers helps us to lower our carbon footprint. We provide jobs and an important boost for the national economy.

They would prefer that part of the home page to look like this:

CS Cressida Snacks provide quality tasty snacks across the country. We have a range of products and flavours which are low in sugar. Ingredients are responsibly sourced and extensive use of local suppliers helps us to lower our carbon footprint. We provide jobs and an important boost for the national economy.

a) Explain the difference in the CSS properties of the image between the two examples shown.

Marks: 2 — Implementation (CSS)

b) One area of the site features a small image from the file TC.png which users can click to show the paragraph of terms and conditions. The paragraph has the id 'terms'.

Show the correct line combining HTML, CSS and JavaScript which will show an image from the file TC.png that when clicked will change the display property of the paragraph with the id terms so that it becomes visible.

Marks: 5 — Implementation (CSS), Implementation (JavaScript)

> **Hint!**
>
> Here the code for your answer will not appear within the paragraph element that is to be styled, so you can't use 'this' as a parameter for a JavaScript function.

c) What would the display property of the terms and conditions paragraph have been set to when the page loaded?

Marks: 1 — Implementation (CSS)

d) Which JavaScript function would be used to hide the paragraph again when the mouse pointer moves off of the button?

Marks: 1 — Implementation (JavaScript)

e) Cressida Snacks have tested the compatibility of their site by ensuring it displays correctly on different types of device, including those with different operating systems.

How else could they test the compatibility of their site?

Marks: 1 — Testing

ANSWERS TO PRACTICE QUESTIONS

Section 1

Software design and development

Question number		Answer	Marks available
1	a)	s=result%60 OR s=result MOD 60 OR s=mod(result, 60)	1
	b)	to ensure the variable is assigned an integer value (and not a real/floating point value)	1
2		First mark, one of: ▶ in agile, regular meetings means client can suggest features before release/early in the process ▶ in agile, use of prototypes means client can suggest features before release/early in the process. Second mark, one of: ▶ in iterative, client might not first use program until after release ▶ in iterative, client can only suggest features at analysis or evaluation stage.	2

3		IF parcel_code(iteration) = target_code THEN
		OR
		IF target_code = parcel_code(iteration) THEN
			1

Computer systems

Question number		Answer	Marks available
1		-1024 to $+1023$ OR $-2^{11}-1$ to $(2^{11}-1)-1$ 1 mark for upper limit. 1 mark for lower limit.	2
2	a)	Any one from: ▶ more transfers to/from (main) memory in a second ▶ greater throughput of instructions ▶ more operations per second.	1
	b)	The speed of the system is limited by another component (examples acceptable, e.g. data bus width).	1
3		Any example where the system acts proactively, e.g. ▶ System may learn times of day/year when traffic is heavy/light/moves predominately in one direction. ▶ System may communicate and coordinate with other nearby traffic lights to reduce stoppages (of traffic).	1
4		Celine has broken the law (1 mark) as she has attempted to gain unauthorised access (to computer material). (1 mark)	2

Question number		Answer	Marks available
5		Any two from: ▸ An individual might have personal reasons to dislike the social network (examples acceptable, e.g. former employee made redundant). ▸ A group may have political reasons to want to target the social network (examples acceptable, e.g. privacy-focused activist groups). ▸ A competitor may wish to affect the social network's ability to function.	2
6	a)	Using the (receiver's) private key	1
	b)	This proves the document is authentic (that Frode created the document) OR this proves no one has changed the document since Frode sent it.	1

Database design and development

Question number		Answer	Marks available
1		 One mark for correct representation of the first relationship. Other answers than that shown are possible as long as each is one to one. One mark for correct representation of the second relationship. Other answers than that shown are possible, as long as at least two employees link to one department.	2
2		<table><tr><th>Type</th><th>Lowest stock level</th></tr><tr><td>print</td><td>12</td></tr><tr><td>office</td><td>9</td></tr></table> 1 mark for correct column headings 'Type' and 'Lowest stock level'. 1 mark for 'print' in the same row as '12'. 1 mark for 'office' in the same row as '9'.	3
3		A compound key is two or more primary keys from other tables (or foreign keys) combined so as to uniquely identify each record in a database. (1 mark) In this example there could be a problem if two staff members have the same job title at the same site. (1 mark)	2
4		Any two from: ▸ database should store every student council/election/candidate for the last 30 years ▸ database should be searchable for candidates on the council in a given year ▸ database should be searchable for number of candidate votes in a given year. Answers beginning 'users should be able to…' or similar are not acceptable, as this is the wording for user requirements, not functional requirements.	2

Web design and development

Question number		Answer	Marks available
1	a)	○ PlayBox ○ Z-Station ○ Button Masher No radio buttons should initially be shown as selected.	1
	b)	`<input type="submit" value="OK">`	1

2		`function changeBG(para)`
		`{para.style.background="yellow";}`
		One mark for naming the function changeBG and having a parameter.
		One mark for changing the background of the parameter to yellow.
		Parameter doesn't need to be called 'para', as long as it isn't called 'this'.
			2

3		 Lines should only meet boxes where shown. One mark for correct first level showing home page linking to T-shirts, Mugs and Publications. One mark for correctly showing four sub-pages from Publications as shown.	2
4		An expert/young person/someone used to using mobile devices. (1 mark) A novice/elderly person/someone unfamiliar with using a mobile device. (1 mark)	2
5		The display property is set to none so the text/paragraph will disappear.	1

Section 2

Software design and development

Question number		Answer	Marks available
1	a)	Any two from: ▸ The program will only deal with levels of carbon dioxide (and not any other substance). ▸ The program will only deal with measurements on Earth. ▸ The program will only deal with measurements from the last 40 years.	2
	b)	▸ Analysis stage could be the only meeting with the client before the project is completed. ▸ These inform all other stages of the development process. For the second bullet point an example of a **stage** and **how the analysis affects that stage** is acceptable, e.g. developers need a complete and concise statement of the problem in order to plan the solution at the design stage.	2
	c)	 1 mark for 'Open file'. 1 mark for 'Loop 40 times'. 1 mark for reading both data items from file into separate arrays. 1 mark for 'Close file'. 1 mark for correct data flow (it would not be wrong to show 'file name' flowing into the 'Open file' step if you have assumed the file name is stored in a variable).	5
1	d)	Either one of: ▸ local ▸ code within the `findAve` function/subprogram.	1
	e)	First mark, one of: ▸ Line 3 doesn't say what to do with the result returned by the function. ▸ The function accepts only one parameter/line 3 passes in two parameters. Second mark, `SET aveReading TO findAve(reading)` or `aveReading = findAve(reading)`	2

Question number		Answer	Marks available

	f)	```SET maxPosition TO 0```
		 ```FOR index FROM 1 TO 39 DO```
		   ```IF reading(index)>reading(maxPosition) THEN```
		    ```SET maxPosition TO index```
		   ```END IF```
		 ```END FOR```
		 ```SEND "Highest was " & reading(maxPosition) " ppm in " &```
		 ```year(maxPosition) TO DISPLAY```
		 1 mark for initialising variable to zero.
		 1 mark for looping 39 times and ending that loop.
		 1 mark for correct ```IF``` and ```END IF```.
		 1 mark for storing new maximum.
		 1 mark for displaying results correctly.
			5

	g)	```SET choice TO CHR((ASC(choice)-32))``` 1 mark for correct use of ```ASC```. 1 mark for correct use of ```CHR```. 1 mark for subtracting 32 in the correct place. It is possible to solve this using two or three lines of code and additional variables; this would not be penalised.	3
2	a)	▸ In iterative, each team works independently of the other teams, with little communication between them. ▸ In agile, separate teams communicate often to share skills/share ideas/clarify requirements.	2
	b)	Effective use of subprograms/subroutines/procedures/functions	1
	c)	Dry run	1
	d)	The design is fit for purpose (1 mark) as it will find and display all occurrences of a user's login. (1 mark) The design does not make efficient use of coding constructs (1 mark) as there is no need to loop round the data twice. (1 mark)	4

	e)	```FOR index FROM 0 TO 34 DO```
		   ```SET username(index) TO Left(surname(index),4) &```
		 ```Left(forename(index),3)```
		 ```END FOR```
		 Line 2 could also be ```SET username(index) TO Mid(surname(index),1,4) & Mid(forename(index),1,3)```
		 or ```SET username(index) TO surname(index) [0:4] & forename(index) [0:3]```
		 (at time of going to print, substring is not yet included in SQA Reference Language)
		 1 mark for beginning and ending ```FOR``` loop 35 times.
		 1 mark for correct use of index variable for all three arrays.
		 1 mark for correct substring of both surname and forename.
			3

	f)	1 mark for Robustness is how well a program copes with errors during execution. Second mark for any of: ▸ input validation ▸ testing with exceptional data ▸ usability testing has test cases for every feature in the program.	2

Question number		Answer	Marks available
3	a)	Accept the following inputs: name (of object), length, breadth. (1 mark) Calculate area. (1 mark) Draw/show rectangle on screen. (1 mark) Show the following outputs: name (of object), length, breadth, area. (1 mark)	4
	b)	Any three from: ▸ design of the solution ▸ test plan and test table ▸ program code ▸ test runs/results of testing ▸ evaluation of the solution.	3
	c)	1. Get inputs from user (out: name, length, breadth). 2. Calculate area (in: length, breadth; out: area). 3. Show rectangle graphic (in: length, breadth). 4. Show text outputs (in: name, length, breadth, area). 1 mark for each correct step.	4
	d)	The program will pause at a specific line of code (1 mark) allowing Morven to compare the values of the variables against expected values. (1 mark)	2
	e)	Morven could use a watchpoint (1 mark) to pause every time the area is changed/accessed (1 mark) (as it may be being changed elsewhere in the program).	2

Computer systems

Question number		Answer	Marks available
1	a)	Any one of: ▸ The system makes a decision based on input from sensors. ▸ The system learns from previous experience.	1
	b)	Ensure the embedded CPU has multiple cores (1 mark) in order to process simultaneous inputs from sensors/user. (1 mark)	2
	c)	▸ Address of the instruction is placed on the address bus. ▸ Read line (on the control bus) is activated. ▸ Contents of the memory location (instruction) are transferred to a register/the CPU along data bus. ▸ Instruction is decoded/executed. 3 marks for all four steps in the correct order. 2 marks for three steps in the correct order OR four steps in an incorrect order. 1 mark for two steps in the correct order OR three steps in an incorrect order. 0 marks for any other response.	3
	d)	Either one of: ▸ more operations per second ▸ higher throughput of instructions.	1

Question number		Answer	Marks available
	e)	Any two from: ▸ Individuals may access the system without permission. ▸ Individuals may access the system without permission with the intent to commit a further crime (for example, to record a user's movements/whereabouts in order to rob their home). ▸ Individuals may access the system without permission and change/delete data/ settings (for example, dramatically reduce the engine's ability to function by altering fuel injection/air flow).	2
	f)	Either one of: ▸ lost revenue from customers being unable to access services ▸ paying staff to fix the fault/vulnerability.	1

Database design and development

Question number		Answer	Marks available
1	a)	Any one from: ▸ activities that the user wishes to be able to carry out ▸ features the user wishes to have ▸ data the user wishes to be present.	1
	b)	None of the tables contains a foreign key.	1
	c)	Range (1 mark) > 0 (1 mark)	2
	d)	`SELECT SUM([Area in m²]) FROM Site AS "Total Area";` 1 mark for `SELECT SUM([Area in m²])` 1 mark for `FROM Site` 1 mark for `AS "Total Area";`	3
2	a)	 1 mark for each correct cardinality (one Ingredient to many Farm, one Ingredient to many Order Line, one Caterer to many Order Line).	3
	b)	`UPDATE Ingredient SET [Bought For] = [Bought For] + 0.01 WHERE [Farm Name]="Tiston"` 1 mark for `UPDATE Ingredient` 1 mark for `SET [Bought For] = [Bought For] + 0.01` 1 mark for `WHERE [Farm Name]="Tiston"`	3
	c)	First mark for it will generate an error. Second mark for either of: ▸ the syntax is incorrect ▸ it should be `DELETE * FROM Ingredient WHERE Name="Pea";`	2
	d)	The output is accurate (1 mark) as the (actual) result of the SQL statement will match the expected result. (1 mark)	2

Question number		Answer	Marks available
	e)	<table><tr><td>**Field(s) and calculation(s)**</td><td>`count(Order ID)`</td></tr><tr><td>**Table(s) and query**</td><td>`Order Line`</td></tr><tr><td>**Search criteria**</td><td></td></tr><tr><td>**Grouping**</td><td>`Ingredient Name`</td></tr><tr><td>**Sort order**</td><td></td></tr></table> 1 mark for each correct entry in the table.	3
	f)	`INSERT INTO Farm VALUES ("Jiri Plasil", "Sudbury", "555 6777");` 1 mark for `INSERT INTO Farm` 1 mark for `VALUES ("Jiri Plasil", "Sudbury", "555 6777");` OR `INSERT INTO Farm (Contact, Name, [Contact Tel])VALUES ("Jiri Plasil", "Sudbury", "555 6777");` is also correct.	2
	g)	<table><tr><th>Ingredient Name</th><th>Quantity</th></tr><tr><td>Strawberry</td><td>162</td></tr><tr><td>Raspberry</td><td>150</td></tr><tr><td>Raspberry</td><td>140</td></tr><tr><td>Raspberry</td><td>100</td></tr></table> 1 mark for including Strawberry with correct Quantity only. 1 mark for showing three entries of Raspberry with correct Quantities only. 1 mark for showing results in descending order of Quantity.	3

Web design and development

Question number		Answer	Marks available
1	a)	banner1.jpg Link to Brass page shop.jpg **About Us** collection.png Link to generate email — Link to Woodwind page — Link to String page — Link to Percussion page 1 mark for three correctly positioned and named images. 1 mark for five correctly positioned and labelled hyperlinks. 1 mark for heading and text beneath.	3
	b)	`main img { height:250px; width:250px; }` 1 mark for `main img` 1 mark for `height:250px; width:250px` Be careful to specify the units as px.	2
	c)	`nav:hover {color:red }` 1 mark for `nav:hover` 1 mark for `{color:red;}`	2
	d)	Between `<style>` and `</style>`. (1 mark) In the `head` section. (1 mark)	2
	e)	The new paragraph will appear on the same line as the text within the existing paragraph.	1
	f)	The new paragraph will appear on a different line from the text within the existing paragraph (possibly with padding around it).	1
	g)	`header, main, footer {margin-top:5px; margin-bottom:5px;}` 1 mark for `header, main, footer` 1 mark for `{margin-top:5px; margin-bottom:5px;}`	2

Question number		Answer	Marks available
	h)	Either one of: ▸ aids usability (of the web page) ▸ aids readability (of the paragraph text).	1
2	a)	The image in the current version of the page has the float property set to none. (1 mark) The image in the desired version of the page has the float property set to left. (1 mark)	2

	b)	`<img src="TC.png" onClick="document.getElementById('terms').style.display= 'block' " >`
		OR
		`<img src="TC.png" onClick="document.getElementById('terms').style.display= 'inline' " >`
		1 mark for `img src="TC.png"`
		1 mark for using `onClick`
		1 mark for using `document.getElementById`
		1 mark for use of correct id `'terms'`
		1 mark for `.style.display= 'block'` or `.style.display= 'inline'`
			5

	c)	none	1
	d)	`onmouseout`	1
	e)	on different browsers	1

PRACTICE PAPER 1

Total Marks: 25

Attempt **ALL** questions.

There is no strict allocation of time for each section; however, each paper should be complete in 2 hours 30 minutes as this is the length of time for the SQA Higher papers.

MARKS

1 Convert the denary number −92 into binary using 8-bit two's complement.   1

2 Kevin has written a program that involves storing text files. State one reason why the use of Unicode might be preferable to extended ASCII for storage of text.   1

_____

_____

3 A real number is stored using 32-bit floating point representation. The mantissa is allocated 8 bits and 24 bits are allocated to the exponent. Describe the effect if the allocation is changed to a 16-bit mantissa and a 16-bit exponent.   2

_____

_____

_____

_____

4 Part of a program that calculates total annual rainfall is shown below. The code makes use of a function to add up a total of four numbers: 1

Line 1: `RECEIVE autumn FROM keyboard`

Line 2: `RECEIVE winter FROM keyboard`

Line 3: `RECEIVE spring FROM keyboard`

Line 4: `RECEIVE summer FROM keyboard`

Line 5: `SET total_rainfall TO total(autumn, winter, spring, summer)`

The code shown makes use of arguments. Explain what is meant by an argument.

_____

_____

_____

MARKS

5 Simon is undertaking the analysis of a new problem submitted by a client. One technique Simon will use to clarify the client's requirements is interviewing the client. Describe two other techniques that Simon could use to better understand the client's requirements.

2

_____

_____

_____

_____

6 The entity-occurrence diagram below shows data on the structure of government for a small country:

2

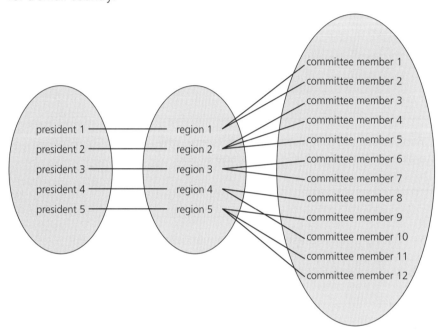

State the cardinality of the relationships shown in the entity-occurrence diagram.

_____

_____

7 Anne has been collating player data from her town's local handball league. Part of her database looks like this:

Player				
playerID	Forename	Surname	Team	Goals
01	Dara	Kilney	North	165
02	Fiona	Smith	East	176
03	Jennifer	Lyle	West	179
04	Delia	Naughton	East	166
05	Orsi	Nagy	South	170
06	Karyn	Waugh	North	175
07	Fiona	Smith	South	183
08	Celia	Thauvin	West	177
09	Lakshmi	Patel	West	175
10	Samantha	Jones	North	181
11	Sharon	Du Pont	East	166
12	Myla	Sinna	South	170
13	Pauline	Urquhart	East	171
14	Linda	Hall	West	170
15	Stephanie	Vannini	North	178
16	Christina	Nkawali	East	181
17	Erica	Svensson	North	178
18	Iris	Thompson	West	175
19	Claudia	Tervet	South	177
20	Andrea	North	South	176

2

Anne wishes to run a query to show the name of each team and the total number of goals that team scored. Complete the design below to produce this result. The second row has been completed for you.

Field(s) and calculation(s)	
Table(s) and query	Player
Search criteria	
Grouping	
Sort order	

8 A local restaurant wants to have an app created for customers to order and pay for food.

a) Suggest a scenario that could be part of the usability testing for this app.

_____

_____

1

b) Explain how a low-fidelity prototype could be used in testing the app.

_____

_____

_____

1

9 Below is part of a program which checks that the correct password has been entered before showing an account balance.

Line 1: `REPEAT`
Line 2: `  RECEIVE password FROM keyboard`
Line 3: `UNTIL password = correct_password`
Line 4: `SEND balance TO DISPLAY`

Explain the impact of cache on the execution of lines 3 and 4.

_____

_____

_____

_____

2

10 Electronic communications are often kept secure during transmission through use of public and private keys. Explain why having access to a company's public key does not help criminals to access any communications they have intercepted from customers to the company.

_____

_____

1

11 Nordin Applications prefer to create programs using an agile design methodology. They have just created a prototype version with some working features. Explain why the term 'agile' is used to describe this kind of methodology.

_____

_____

1

12 Nile is an online shopping company. They are designing a version of their website to work well on mobile devices.

a) Describe two considerations that should be taken into account when designing a website for display on mobile devices.

_____

_____

_____

_____

2

b) One page of the site includes a form for ordering products. The following HTML code is used to allow input of the quantity to be added to the order:

`Quantity:`
`<input type="number" name="quantity">`

Nile has decided to limit the number of any item that a customer can order to 30. Rewrite the code so that the quantity that can be ordered is restricted to between 1 and 30 inclusive.

1

13 Anita has written a program that makes use of a procedure to convert miles into kilometres.

Program:
```
DECLARE miles, km AS REAL
SEND "Enter number of miles" TO DISPLAY
RECEIVE miles FROM KEYBOARD
convert(miles, km)
SEND "That is " & km & " kilometres" TO DISPLAY
```

Procedure:
```
PROCEDURE convert(REAL x, REAL y)
   SET y TO x * 1.60934
END PROCEDURE
```

Identify one formal parameter from the code above and explain what a formal parameter is.

_____

_____

_____

14 Hidetoshi's program uses parallel arrays and pre-defined functions.

a) Which attribute of parallel one-dimensional arrays must be the same?

_____

b) Explain what is meant by a pre-defined function.

_____

_____

_____

[End of Section 1]

MARKS

15 An app that contains a game has been created and includes a high-score table stored in a separate sequential file called 'scores.txt'. Every time the game is played the high-score table is shown, updated and saved if appropriate at the end of the game.

a) Using pseudocode, or a programming language with which you are familiar, complete the code below to read 10 names and high scores from the file into the arrays name[] and score[]:

2

```
_____

FOR counter FROM 0 TO 9 DO

   _____

   _____

END FOR

_____
```

The creators of the app chose to use a .txt file rather than a .csv file.

b) State one difference between a .csv file and a .txt file.

1

_____

_____

The game allows users to play with a group of three game characters, each with a different name and a different rating for their strength, magic, speed and intelligence.

The game code features the record structure shown to allow this:

```
RECORD adventurer IS {STRING name, INTEGER strength,
INTEGER magic, INTEGER speed, INTEGER intelligence}
```

c) The programmer wants to store the three adventurers' data using the record structure shown above. The array is to be named `party[]`.

Using pseudocode, or a programming language of your choice, declare the array which can store the data for the three game characters.

2

The first character's details are shown below:

name	Grek
strength	19
magic	3
speed	6
intelligence	4

d) Using pseudocode, or a programming language of your choice, write the code necessary to add the data for the adventurer shown in the above table.

Your answer should use the array declared in part **b)**.

3

MARKS

When displaying a summary of a character, the following code is used to show the character name and the overall rating. The record for the character being displayed has been assigned to the variable `current`. The overall rating is calculated as the average of the four integer fields:

```
Line 1  DECLARE overall AS INTEGER
Line 2  overall = (current.strength + current.magic +
current.speed + current.intelligence)/4
Line 3  SEND "Name: " & current.name TO KEYBOARD
Line 4  SEND "Overall Rating: " & overall TO KEYBOARD
```

e) (i) Describe the kind of error that may occur as a result of line 2.

1

_____

_____

_____

(ii) Describe two ways that the above code could be changed to prevent an error from occurring when line 2 is executed.

2

_____

_____

_____

_____

The app was tested on a mobile phone released two weeks ago and it performed as expected.

f) Describe two problems that may be encountered when testing the app on a mobile phone released three years ago.

2

_____

_____

_____

_____

16 Kyle is using a database to keep track of music releases. The database has four linked tables, shown below:

Band	Band ID	PK
	Name	

Member	Member ID	PK
	Name	
	Band ID	FK

Album	Album ID	PK
	Name	
	Band ID	FK

Song	Song ID	PK
	Name	
	Album ID	FK
	Peak Chart Position	

a) Complete the entity-relationship diagram below.

6

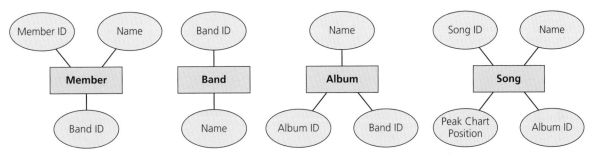

Below is a partially complete data dictionary for the database:

Entity	Attribute	Key	Data type/size	Unique	Required	Validation
Band	Band ID	PK	Text (12)			
	Name		Text (50)			
Member	Member ID	PK	Text (8)		2.	
	Name		Text (60)			
	Band ID	FK	Text (12)			
Album	Album ID	PK	Text (10)	1.		
	Name		Text (100)			
	Band ID	FK	Text (12)			
Song	Song ID	PK	Text (10)			
	Name		Text (100)			
	Album ID	FK	Text (10)			3.
	Peak Chart Position		Number			

b) Indicate what you would expect to be contained in the missing entries **1.**, **2.** and **3.**

2

1. _____

2. _____

3. _____

c) Kyle would like to see the best peak chart position achieved by each band. Write the SQL statement that would produce this result. The result is shown here:

5

Name	Best Peak Chart Position
Amazon Penguins	2
Contemplate Wyverns	4
Kings of the Iron Age	9
Big Churn	1
Fourth Melody	1

d) Kyle's friend has made a query containing the following SQL:

2

```
SELECT Album.Name, Count([Song ID])
FROM Album, Song
WHERE Song.[Album ID]=Album.[Album ID]
GROUP BY Album.Name;
```

Describe the effect of running the query.

_____

_____

_____

17 Gillian has designed a website for a charity that employs staff to provide support to young carers (young people who care for members of their family).

Gillian intends to use a horizontal navigation bar at the top of each page of the site. She has included the hyperlinks to the four main sections:

```
<a href="cz.html">Carer's Zone</a> |
<a href="about.html">About Us</a> |
<a href="contact.html">Get in Contact</a> |
<a href="/resources/">Resources</a>
```

a) (i) Which HTML code should appear around the links to ensure they make up the navigation bar?   **1**

(ii) Which HTML code should your answer to part (i) appear within to indicate that it should appear at the top of each page of the site?   **1**

One page of the site uses a web form to allow users get in contact with the charity. The HTML code for the form is shown below:

```
<form id="contact">
First name:<br>
<input type="text" name="firstname" size="30"> <br><br>
Last name:<br>
<input type="text" name="lastname" size="30"> <br><br>
Email address:<br>
<input type="text" name="email" size="60">
<input type="submit" value="Submit">
</form>
<br>
Comment: <br>
<textarea name="comment" rows="30" cols="120"
form="contact">
</textarea>
```

b) (i) Explain what change could be made to the above HTML code to validate the length of the first name to be 25 characters or fewer.   **1**

(ii) Explain what change could be made to the above HTML to ensure that an email address had to be entered and that this could not be left blank.   **1**

(iii) The `<textarea>` tag appears after the `</form>` tag. Explain how the browser knows that data entered into this text area relates to the above form.   **2**

Another section of the site features an ordered list followed by an unordered list. The HTML code for this section is show below:

```
<p>We exist to help:
<ol>
<li>Young carers</li>
<li>Parents/guardians of young carers</li>
<li>People being cared for by young carers</li>
</ol>
Please feel free to
<ul>
   <li>Call us</li>
   <li>Email us</li>
   <li>Pop in and see us</li>
</ul></p>
```

c) Using descendant selectors write CSS rules to show all ordered list items in blue text and all unordered list items in red text.

2

_____

_____

The charity is concerned about high utility bills caused by the heating system being switched on from early morning until late evening. This is because the different staff members and young people come and go from the offices at different times.

They are considering installing an intelligent heating system that will reduce bills and help the environment.

d) Explain how an intelligent heating system can help the environment.

1

_____

_____

18 A client has asked CalumCorp to develop a program. Andy is part of a team developing a program using an agile computing methodology.

a) Describe two advantages of this development methodology for the client.

2

_____

_____

_____

_____

b) As part of the program it must include a section to find the total of any valid number in a list of three numbers. Valid numbers are 0 and above. An incomplete part of the test plan for this section is shown below:

	first number	second number	third number	expected total	actual total
Test 1	7	3	2	12	
Test 2	2	9	**X**		
Test 3	4	**Y**	5		

Write down two different suitable values to be entered in place of the **X** and **Y** indicated in the table and explain your choice for each.

_____

_____

_____

_____

Andy has created this section in the program:

```
Line 1  DECLARE numberArray INITIALLY [7,3,2]
Line 2  DECLARE total INITIALLY 0
Line 3  FOR EACH number FROM numberArray DO
Line 4    IF number >= 0 THEN
Line 5      SET total TO total + number
Line 6    END IF
Line 7  END FOR
Line 8  SEND total TO DISPLAY
```

(c) Andy now wants to store the highest valid number in a variable called `max`. He has to add four new lines in the spaces indicated in order to do this:

```
Line 1  DECLARE numberArray INITIALLY [7,3,2]
Line 2  DECLARE total INITIALLY 0
Line 3  _____
Line 4  FOR EACH number FROM numberArray DO
Line 5    IF number >= 0 THEN
Line 6      SET total TO total + number
Line 7      _____
Line 8      _____
Line 9      _____
Line 10   END IF
Line 11 END FOR
Line 12 SEND total TO DISPLAY
```

Using a programming language of your choice, write the four missing lines of code.

2

MARKS

19 Clarissa works for Dunton Juniors football club. She is writing a program to analyse data held on season ticket holders at the club.

The program includes an array of integers called `age[]` to hold the age that each season ticket holder was when they bought their current season ticket. Clarissa wants the program to use this array and show on screen how many season ticket holders are under the age of 18.

a) Show, using pseudocode or a programming language that you are familiar with, how she would do this.

5

b) Customers pay for their tickets on the Dunton Juniors website. However, because this is a small local business, some customers are concerned when they log on to the site that they are not on the genuine Dunton Juniors website. Explain how Dunton Juniors could reassure those customers.

2

_____

_____

_____

_____

c) The website uses asymmetric encryption to ensure that login and payment data are secure through the use of a public key and a private key. Explain the steps involved in Dunton Juniors' website securely receiving data from a user using this.

2

_____

_____

_____

_____

MARKS

d) The site home page contains the following CSS:

4

```
p: { margin-top:4px; margin-bottom: 4px; padding: 9px; }
footer: { margin-top:8px; margin-bottom: 5px; padding:
9px; }
header: { margin-top:8px; margin-bottom: 5px; padding:
9px; }
img: { margin-top:4px; margin-bottom: 4px; padding: 9px;
}
main: { margin-top:6px; margin-bottom: 6px; padding:
9px;  }
```

Using grouping selectors to remove any repetition, rewrite the code to make it more efficient.

e) Suggest two test cases that could be used during testing of the Dunton Juniors website and give a reason for each suggestion.

2

_____

_____

_____

_____

20 Grace is designing a website for a firm that sells vehicles. From the home page users should be able to choose whether to go to a page about vans for sale or a page about cars for sale. From the page selling vans, customers should then be able to go to a page to search for new vans or a page to search for used vans. Similarly, from the page selling cars, customers should then be able to go to a page to search for new cars or a page to search for used cars.

a) Design a multilevel structure for the vehicle sales website.

2

Part of the home page contains the following HTML:

```
<h1>Findlay Vehicles</h1>
<img src="logo.gif" width="100" height="132">
<p class="introduction">Findlay Vehicles sell high quality
new and used vehicles both online and from our various
locations in Scotland</p>
<p class="locations">You can find us in Hillington, Wester
Hailes, Broughty Ferry and Bridge of Don</p>
```

Grace would like to ensure that all images on the home page appear at the left of their section.

b) Write a CSS rule to make images appear at the left of their section.

_____

1

Following the inclusion of a CSS rule to have images appear at the left of their section, the image appears to the left of both paragraphs on the home page. Grace has been asked to have the logo only next to the introduction paragraphs and not next to the locations paragraph.

c) Write a CSS rule to ensure no images or other elements appear beside the locations paragraph on either side.

_____

2

d) The site includes many image files that are photographs of vehicles. Explain why a bitmap file type must be used to store these.

_____

_____

1

21 Malala is using a desktop computer to develop a new app for mobile devices.

Rehman has told Malala that it is easier to code the program using global variables. However, Malala makes use of parameter passing instead.

a) Describe two risks that Rehman takes in always using global variables in his code.

_____

_____

_____

_____

2

b) Malala has used some procedures and some functions. Explain how procedures are different from functions.

_____

_____

_____

2

c) The app features diagrams stored as vector graphics. Explain why this method is more suitable than bitmap storage for an app designed for mobile devices.

_____

_____

_____

2

d) The app stores details of concert venues for hire. It holds the names and hire costs and the maximum number of people the venue can hold. These are stored in three parallel one-dimensional arrays called `venue[]`, `price[]` and `capacity[]`.

Malala wants to add a subprogram so that a target cost is passed in and it returns the position of the highest capacity venue that can be hired for that target cost or less.

Using a recognised design technique, design this function.

22 Three charities do vital work to help their local communities. Each charity arranges various events which need to be staffed. Each staff member could work or volunteer at more than one charity's events. This information has been stored in a database:

Event				
Event ID	Event Name	Location	Charity ID*	Staff ID*
E001	Kids Art	Beachfront College	C002	S002, S004
E002	Park Walk	Dean Park	C001	S003, S006, S007
E003	Teen Makeup	Magnum High School	C002	S001, S005
E004	Saturday Football	Kay Park	C001	S001, S002, S007
E005	Weekly Food Bank	Burgh Hall	C003	S003, S004

Charity		
Charity ID	Charity Name	Location
C001	PDAB	East Ayrshire
C002	We Care Scotland	North Ayrshire
C003	Storehouse Food Bank	Glasgow

Staff		
Staff ID	Forename	Surname
S001	Karen	Sparrow
S002	Lesley	Brown
S003	David	Turner
S004	Reuben	Crossan
S005	Hayden	Coulter
S006	Alice	Hall
S007	Karen	Killen

a)   Show the entity-occurrence diagram for the state of the database shown above.   2

MARKS

b) Write the correct SQL statement to show a list of all Event Names for events run by a charity that is based in Ayrshire.

4

c) A report is produced from this database that looks like this:

3

> Karen Sparrow your upcoming events are:
> Teen Makeup at Magnum High School for We Care Scotland
> Saturday Football at Kay Park for PDAB

State the tables, fields and criteria used to produce the above report.

_____

_____

_____

_____

d) Which aggregate function would be needed to add the following line to the above report in part **c)**?

1

> Number of upcoming events: 2

_____

[End of Section 1]

[END OF PRACTICE PAPER 1]

PRACTICE PAPER 2

MARKS

1 Two's complement can be used to represent both positive and negative numbers. State the highest positive number and the lowest negative number that can be represented using 12-bit two's complement representation.

2

_____

_____

2 Gerry is following an iterative design methodology. Gerry's program has just reached the testing stage of the software development process. Explain why the term 'iterative' is used to describe this kind of design methodology.

2

_____

_____

3 Convert 110.00011 to floating point representation. There are 16 bits for the mantissa and 8 bits for the exponent.

3

sign	mantissa	exponent

4 One method for improving system performance is the use of cache memory. Explain how the use of cache would speed up the execution of the following code which calculates the volume of a room:

2

```
SET roof_height TO peak_height - wall_height
SET lower_volume TO wall_height * length * width
SET upper_volume TO (roof_height * length * width) / 3
SET room_volume TO lower_volume + upper_volume
```

_____

_____

_____

_____

5 Gina runs a database for a charity, and wishes to use a SQL statement to delete an entire table called 'Volunteer' from her database as it is no longer needed. Graham suggests the following statement:

3

```
DELETE * FROM Volunteer;
```

Evaluate the fitness for purpose of the above SQL statement. Justify your answer.

_____

_____

_____

_____

6 Stephanie has created an external CSS stylesheet called 'webstyle'. Complete the HTML code that will successfully link to this stylesheet:

2

```
<_____ rel ="stylesheet" _____= "text/css"
href="webstyle.css">
```

7 A radio station is creating a program to store details about songs. The details stored are: track name, artist name and highest chart position.

2

   a) Using a programming language of your choice, define a suitable record structure to store the necessary song details.

   b) Using a programming language of your choice, define the variable that can store the data for 5000 songs. Your answer should use the record structure created in part **a)**.

2

8 Tiana's program features constructs, variables and subprograms.

   a) Explain what is meant by the scope of a variable.

1

   b) Explain how programmers determine the scope of a variable.

1

9 Christopher has included a form in his web page to allow users to select the flavour of ice cream that they like. He has used the following HTML code:

```
<select name="flavour">
  <option value="vanilla">Vanilla</option>
  <option value="chocolate">Chocolate</option>
  <option value="strawberry">Strawberry</option>
  <option value="mintcc">Mint Choc Chip</option>
  <option value="pistachio">Pistachio</option>
</select>
```

Currently users can only select one flavour from the drop-down menu, and the drop-down menu shows only the flavour selected when a menu choice has been made:

Describe how Christopher could change the HTML so that users can see all five options at once, and can select multiple flavours at the same time:

_____

_____

_____

10 Clark has included the following HTML and JavaScript on a web page:

```
<img class="teamImage" src="official.jpg" onmouseover="this.
src='celebrate.jpg' " onmouseout="this.src='official.jpg' ">
```

Explain the effect of the above HTML and JavaScript.

_____

_____

_____

_____

_____

_____

[End of Section 1]

Section 2

Total Marks: 85

Attempt **ALL** questions.

11 Fleur is a company that makes and sells packs of tea bags of various flavours of tea. They have a desktop application that allows them to keep track of their sales.

For each type of tea, the number of packs sold that week is stored in an array called `sold[]`, and the name of the type of tea is stored in an array called `name[]`:

name	jasmine	cinnamon	camomile	dusk	pink	autumn	green	detox
sold	18	16	15	16	65	65	30	3

a) The sales statistics feature allows the user to enter a type of tea, and displays a message, e.g.

`The number of sales of dusk was 16`

Write, using pseudocode or a language with which you are familiar, an algorithm that can:

- find the number of sales for the type of tea entered by the user
- display a similar message to that shown above, or an error message if that type is not in the list.

The type of tea entered by the user will be held in a variable called `target_name`.

6

b) The following code is used with the `sold[]` array as shown above to calculate the sales per week:

```
DECLARE total AS INTEGER INITIALLY 0
FOR product FROM 0 TO 7 DO
   SET total TO total + sold[product]
   SEND total TO DISPLAY
END FOR
```

Part of a trace table is shown below. The trace table shows the values at the end of each iteration of the loop.

Entries **(i)** and **(ii)** are missing. Complete these entries.

product	0	1	2	3
sold	18	16	15	16
total	18	34	**(i)**	**(ii)**

2

c) Fleur has decided to stop selling the 'detox' type of tea due to poor sales, and the array now contains this data for the following week:

name	jasmine	cinnamon	camomile	dusk	pink	autumn	green
sold	19	26	14	19	60	47	39

2

However, this change results in an error when the programmer runs the code from part **b)**.

Explain why the error occurs and what change could be made to the code to correct the error.

_____

_____

_____

_____

d) The manager wishes a feature in the program to state how many types of tea sold 30 or more packs in one week.

(i) Which standard algorithm would be applied to the above arrays in order to show that result?

_____

1

(ii) Using the arrays from part **c)**, show, using pseudocode or a language with which you are familiar, the steps to show the number of types of tea for which there were 30 or more sales.

4

e) A function is written as part of the program code. State two attributes of a function that are stated when a function is created.

_____

_____

12 Dani runs a shop in Canada that sells goods such as toiletries and confectionary imported from Scotland. She decides to keep track of this information in a database with four tables:

Product	Product ID	PK
	Name	
	Description	
	Category	FK
	Manufacturer	FK

Category	Name	PK
	Description	
	Current Discount	

Manufacturer	Manufacturer ID	PK
	Name	
	Address	
	Tel No	
	Exporter	FK

Exporter	Exporter ID	PK
	Name	
	Address	
	Tel No	

a) State the cardinality of the relationships between the four tables above.

_____

_____

_____

Dani's customers can browse her database from a kiosk within the shop. After a customer submits a query, the screen below has been shown:

b) Design the query that has been used to generate the screen on page 53.

Field(s) and calculation(s)	
Table(s) and query	
Search criteria	
Grouping	
Sort order	

Dani is updating the website for her business. She has included the ability to query the database from the website, and the results show in a black and white layout similar to that pictured above.

c) Dani wishes to make the text 'Dani International' stand out in blue whenever the user moves the pointer onto those words.

In the body section, Dani has placed the following:

```
<h1 id="dani" onmouseover="mouseOver()" Dani
International</h1>
```

Write the text needed below this in the body section to cause the heading 'Dani International' to stand out in blue whenever the user moves the pointer over those words.

13 Bereket's program is used to calculate charges for hiring bicycles. The departure and return times are converted to and stored as real numbers, for example 08:30 hours will be converted to and stored as 8.5.

The function below is used to calculate the cost of hire for each bike:

```
Line 1   FUNCTION calcCost(REAL departure, REAL return)
         RETURNS REAL
Line 2     DECLARE hours_hired INITIALLY 0
Line 3     DECLARE total_charge INITIALLY 0
Line 4     SET hours_hired TO return-departure
Line 5     IF hours_hired <= 1 THEN
Line 6       SET total_charge TO 5
Line 7       IF hours_hired <=2 THEN
Line 8         SET total_charge TO 8
Line 9       ELSE
Line 10        SET total_charge TO 12.5
Line 11      END IF
Line 12    END IF
Line 13    RETURN total_charge
Line 14 END FUNCTION
```

MARKS

This function is called using the line below:

```
SET cost TO calcCost(left, back)
```

a) Name an actual parameter from the code shown, and describe what is meant by an actual parameter.

2

_____

_____

_____

_____

b) Elena notices errors when testing Bereket's program. If the bike has been hired for more than one hour but less than or equal to two, the cost wrongly shows as zero.

   (i) What cost will show if the bike was hired at 10:00 and returned at 10:30?

1

_____

   (ii) State how to change the above code to remove the errors.

1

_____

c) Elena made use of a breakpoint while testing the program. Explain how a breakpoint is used.

2

_____

_____

_____

_____

d) The calling program contains a variable called `hours_hired`. Explain why this variable is unaffected by the `hours_hired` variable contained within the above `calcCost` function.

1

_____

_____

The information on the money made for each day of the year is held in a text file. A sample of the data in the text file is shown below:

```
12/10/19, 320
13/10/19, 230
14/10/19, 64.5
```

The hire company reads this data into two parallel one-dimensional arrays: an array with the data type string called `date[]` and an array with the data type real called `profit[]`.

One part of the program shows the number of days that the profit was £100 or more. The algorithm used is shown:

1. Import financial data.
2. Count the number of days with profit of 100 or more.
3. Show the number of days with profit of 100 or more.

e) The table below has the data flow completed for steps 1 and 3 of the algorithm. Complete the missing data flow for step 2.

Step	IN/OUT	Data flow
1	IN	
	OUT	date[ ], profit[ ]
2	IN	
	OUT	
3	IN	total
	OUT	

The hire company wants to change the format of the dates stored in the date[ ] array to ensure four characters for the year. They want the characters '2' and '0' inserted in the appropriate place in each entry. For example, an entry that reads '23/11/19' should be changed to '23/11/2019'.

f) Using a programming language of your choice, write the algorithm to update the date formats of all 365 entries in the date[ ] array.

14 Alford Kits sells sports equipment through a database-driven website. One page generated by the website and displayed on a client's browser is shown below:

a) Describe the benefits of performing usability testing on the above website.

b) Two ideas for Alford Kits' latest cricket bat design are shown below:

Design 1   Design 2

The two designs are identical apart from the position of the black oval.

(i) Explain how Design 1 would be changed to Design 2 using a bitmapped graphics package.

_____

_____

1

(ii) Explain how Design 1 would be changed to Design 2 using a vector graphics package.

_____

_____

1

c) The original cricket bat design currently on sale looks like this:

Original design

(i) Explain the difference, if any, in file size from this design to the new designs shown above in part **b)** if the files were all saved as vector graphics.

_____

_____

_____

2

(ii) Explain the difference, if any, in file size from this design to the new designs shown above in part **b)** if the files were all saved as bitmapped graphics.

_____

_____

_____

2

15 Jiong is creating a program to process weather statistics for each of Scotland's 32 local authorities.

He has decided that using a record structure is the best way to do this. He has added the following record structure:

```
RECORD council IS {STRING name, REAL annual_rainfall,
INTEGER hours_sunshine, REAL average_windspeed}
```

He went on to declare an array of records using:

```
DECLARE authority[31] AS council
```

a) Jiong wishes to read in the data for the 32 entries from a text file called 'stats.txt'. Show, using pseudocode or a programming language that you are familiar with, how he would do this.

4

b) Renewable energy can be produced by wind turbines. Jiong wishes to use the data he has within the program to determine the name of the local authority that has the highest average windspeed.

2

His friend Rebekah has written the following function, which she suggests he use within his program:

```
FUNCTION findHighest (ARRAY OF INTEGER list) RETURNS
INTEGER
   DECLARE highest AS INTEGER INITIALLY list[0]
   FOR index FROM 1 TO 31 DO
     IF list[index]>highest THEN
        SET highest TO list[index]
     END IF
   END FOR
   RETURN highest
END FUNCTION
```

Describe two reasons why Jiong cannot use the function as it is shown to find the name of the local authority with the highest average windspeed.

16 Paterson Dirt Moto is a business allowing customers to take motorised dirt bike lessons at various locations around the UK. Each venue features a number of dirt bike tracks and trails, varying in difficulty.

A database has been set up to keep track of the relevant information:

Venue	Name	
	Description	
	Address	
	Venue Postcode	PK
	Tel. No.	

Track	Track Name	PK
	Description	
	Difficulty	
	Venue Postcode	FK
	Image	

Booking	Booking ID	PK
	Venue Postcode	FK
	Date	
	Time	
	No. Riders	
	Customer Name	

Instructor	Instructor ID	PK
	Name	
	Address	
	Tel. No.	
	Venue Postcode	FK

a) Complete the entity-relationship diagram shown for the database above. 5

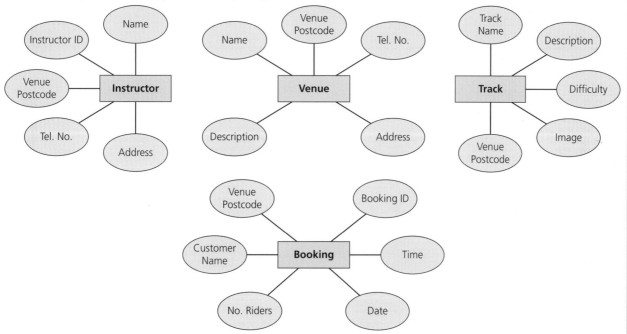

b) Each bike contains a GPS transponder that continually updates the office with the position of the bike as it travels around the track. 2

Explain how the use of a multicore processor could aid in processing the GPS data.

_____

_____

_____

_____

c) A customer has booked with Booking ID 0361 and has asked to add two more riders to the booking. Write the SQL statement to make this change.

3

d) The owners wish to see the total number of riders in 2018 for each venue. The output should look similar to:

6

Name	Total Riders
Bankhead	5760
Deanston	4900
Knockinch	5523
Stillway	5890
Tammick	5628

Write the SQL statement that would produce this result.

17 Artist Neil draws and writes comic books for a living. He has asked a web design company to design a website that can host his artwork and comic books. Users should be able to access selected pieces without logging in. Other artwork or comic books will only be available to premium members who will have a username and password and will pay an annual subscription fee through the website. Neil himself also wishes to be able to log in and upload new artwork or comics, and to decide whether they appear in the free section or the members' section.

a) Identify two functional requirements for the website.

2

Neil has researched wireframes and provided a suggested layout for the login page:

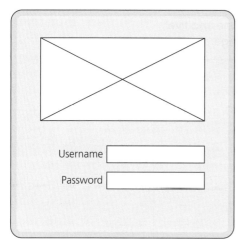

b) Identify two other elements that professional web designers are likely to suggest are added to the wireframe.

2

_____

_____

One page of the website has the following CSS and HTML code applied:

CSS
```
p img {
padding: 70px;
margin-top: 50px;
margin-bottom: 100px;
margin-right: 120px;
margin-left: 85px; }
```

HTML
```
<div><p>
<img src="comicstrip1.jpg">
</p>
<img src="comicstrip2.jpg">
</div>
```

c) (i) How many pixels of space will there be between the end of the image 'comicstrip1.jpg' and the beginning of the image 'comicstrip2.jpg' when displayed in the browser?

1

_____

(ii) Explain the effect that changing the first line of the CSS shown from `p img {` to `div img {` will have on the two images.

4

_____

_____

_____

_____

_____

_____

When viewing comic strips that are results of a search, Neil wants users to be able to choose how many comic strips are shown on each page of results. To do this a small form is needed at the bottom of each page of results.

d) Show the HTML code that will allow users to choose between one and five comic strips per page, to be included at the bottom of every page of results.

5

e) The web designers have completed the website and are undertaking the evaluation stage of the web development process. State one item of documentation that they would require at this stage and explain how it would be used.

1

[End of Section 2]

[END OF PRACTICE PAPER 2]

Practice Paper 1
Section 1

Question			Answer	Marks available	Commentary, hints and tips
1			10100100	1	Positive 92 would be 01011100. Invert the bits to get 10100011. Add 1 to get 10100100. You can always convert it back again to check your answer.
2			Unicode can represent a greater range of characters than ASCII.	1	Unicode uses 16 bits per character so can store 2^{16} (65 536) characters. Extended ASCII only uses 8 bits per character so can only store 2^{8} (256) characters. Answers referring to Unicode being able to represent non-English language characters must still refer to the greater range of characters that can be represented by Unicode.
3			The possible precision will increase. (1 mark) The possible range will decrease. (1 mark)	2	The mantissa part of the floating point number is responsible for the precision of the number. The number of bits for this has increased from 8 to 16, so the number can be more precise. The exponent part of the floating point number is responsible for the range of possible numbers that can be stored. The number of bits for this has decreased from 24 to 16, so the number cannot have as wide a range as before.
4			A variable parameter/data that must be passed into a function/subprogram in order for the function to operate.	1	Most functions require some information to be able to do their job. For example, the LEN ( ) function will return the length of a string. It requires that string to be passed into the function as an argument. In the line `SET length to LEN(name)` the argument is the variable called name.

Question			Answer	Marks available	Commentary, hints and tips
5			Any two from: ▶ Inspect the documentation on the system currently in use. ▶ Observe the system currently in use. ▶ Create a prototype of the solution and ask for feedback from the client.	2	One answer that appears in some textbooks but does not appear in SQA marking guidelines is the issuing of questionnaires, so avoid this answer. The analysis stage is the initial stage in the software development process. Creating the software specification correctly at this early stage will help programmers to be sure that their solution is correct as it is developed at the design and implementation stages. The software specification will form the basis of a legal contract between the client and the programming company, this is another reason why its accuracy is important.
6			President to region is one-to-one. (1 mark) Region to committee member is one-to-many. (1 mark)	2	Cardinality of relationships between entities at Higher level will be one-to-one, one-to-many or many-to-many.
7			<table><tr><td>Field(s) and calculation(s)</td><td>Team, Sum(Goals)</td></tr><tr><td>Table(s) and query</td><td>Player</td></tr><tr><td>Search criteria</td><td></td></tr><tr><td>Grouping</td><td>Team</td></tr><tr><td>Sort order</td><td></td></tr></table> 1 mark for Team, Sum(Goals) in first row, 1 mark for correct grouping.	2	Sum is the aggregate function to add up all the numbers in the field/column. When an aggregate function is used if there is no grouping the result will be one number, the total of all the numbers in that field/column. Here the grouping results in four totals: East 860 North 877 South 876 West 876
8	a)		Any one from: ▶ viewing the menu and making choices ▶ adding payment details ▶ paying the bill ▶ view past orders/payments ▶ any other valid answers.	1	Scenarios are tasks/activities for users to undertake that have a clear goal. Users are told what to do but not how to do it, so that any difficulties that they have are apparent.
	b)		Any one from: ▶ Users use a version of the solution where the interface looks like what developers expect the finished product to look like. ▶ Users are observed and difficulties noted.	1	A low-fidelity prototype is often drawn and put together using pieces of paper or card. The most important element of a low-fidelity prototype is that it is interactive, for usability testing. Usability testing involves giving prospective users a scenario and a list of tasks to perform. Users are observed and also provide feedback by recording problems and suggesting changes.

Question			Answer	Marks available	Commentary, hints and tips
9			Any two from: ▶ Instructions 3/4 will already be (pre-loaded) in cache (i.e. a cache hit will occur). ▶ Data in variable password will already be in cache improving access time/instruction time. ▶ Instruction 4 may never be reached so pre-loading may have no effect.	2	Computer systems will pre-load cache with the upcoming instructions to make fetching them quicker than from slower main memory. However, this can be of no use if the program branches (using an IF). Recently accessed data is also stored in cache. Cache need only be checked for data when attempting to read data from main memory – data stored in registers is already inside the processor. Registers are faster access memory than cache.
10			The private key is required to decrypt data. (1 mark) OR The private key cannot be determined from the public key. (1 mark)	1	When asymmetric encryption is used, the customer's system will have a pair of keys and the company's system will have a pair of keys. The keys in a pair are mathematically related, but one cannot be worked out using the other. The company will release one key to all – this is their public key. Anything encrypted with their public key can then only be decrypted by their private key, so the data is secure. The customer will encrypt data using this public key and send it to the company. The customer will also release one key as a public key. The company can encrypt data using the customer's public key then the customer can decrypt that data when they receive it using the customer's private key.
11			Developers can respond quickly to changes in client demands.	1	In agile methodologies the developers meet often with the clients and seek feedback on prototypes so that their requirements can be changed, thus ensuring the finished product is fit for purpose.
12	a)		Any two from: ▶ text of appropriate colour, size and position to be read ▶ buttons/links/form fields of appropriate size and position to be tapped ▶ embedded videos/graphics of appropriate size and position to be seen clearly on screen ▶ no element overlaps another ▶ scrolling operates as expected.	2	The user interface could be designed using wire framing. The screen on a mobile device is a different size and shape from a computer screen – the size and shape also differ across different kinds of mobile device. Responsive web design involves applying different stylesheets depending on which size of screen the device has.

Question			Answer	Marks available	Commentary, hints and tips
	b)		`<input type="number" name="quantity" min="1" max="30">`	1	When the input type is number then min and max are attributes that can be set to limit the entry into that form element.
13			x or y (1 mark) Second mark, any of: ▶ formal parameter may be a copy of an actual parameter ▶ formal parameter may be a pointer/ placeholder for an actual parameter ▶ formal parameter can be used to control data flow.	2	The formal parameters are the variables as named and used within a subprogram that have been passed in from outside the subprogram. If an actual parameter is passed in by value, the formal parameter will be a copy of the actual parameter which will only exist for the life of the subprogram and will have no effect on the original variable (that is, the actual parameter). If an actual parameter is passed by reference then the formal parameter will contain a pointer to the actual parameter and any change made to the formal parameter will in fact change the actual parameter. Passing by value or reference allows the programmer to control the flow of data.
14	a)		Size/number of elements	1	Parallel arrays require that the data within an array element in one array at a certain index must directly relate to the data contained in the second array at the same index. For example, if the parallel arrays were `name[]` and `age[]`, the person named at `name[4]` should be of the age found in `age[4]`. Consequently, parallel arrays must have the same number of elements as one another.
	b)		It is included with the programming language. (1 mark) It returns a value. (1 mark)	2	'Pre-defined' means that the programmer did not have to code this subprogram, it was already coded and included by the creators of the language. Functions are subprograms that return one value to the calling program/subprogram.

Section 2

Question			Answer	Marks available	Commentary, hints and tips

15	a)		OPEN FILE "scores.txt"
			FOR counter FROM 0 TO 9 DO
			   RECEIVE name(counter) FROM FILE
			   RECEIVE score(counter) FROM FILE
			END FOR
			CLOSE FILE
			1 mark for correct open and close lines,
			1 mark for two correct lines to read contents into array.
				2	The file operations that you may be asked to use are listed by SQA in the Course Assessment Specification: create, open, read, write, close. Be sure to use the file name and array/variable names given in the question.

	b)		CSV will always use a comma as a delimiter/to separate data items in the file.	1	CSV files are saved as plain text (no formatting data is saved) in the same way as .txt files, the file extension .csv only indicates that the creator of the file has used commas between each value in the file, e.g. David,Alford,100.
	c)		DECLARE party[2] As adventurer 1 mark for DIM or DECLARE party[2] 1 mark for As adventurer	2	A record allows a set of variables, with different types, to be named and organised under one data structure. DIM in place of DECLARE would also be acceptable. Be sure to use the array name party[] as this was given in the question. The [2] indicates the array size – this will set up an array of three adventurer records called party[0], party[1] and party[2].
	d)		SET party[0].name TO "Grek" SET party[0].strength TO 19 SET party[0].magic TO 3 SET party[0].speed TO 6 SET party[0].intelligence TO 4 OR DECLARE party[0] INITIALLY adventurer ("Grek", 19, 3, 6, 4) OR SET party[0] TO adventurer ("Grek", 19, 3, 6, 4) 1 mark for use of array from part **c)**, e.g. party[]. 1 mark for use of dot to indicate correct field names. 1 mark for correct entries into fields.	3	The order you will often see is a line to define the record (in this case this is given in the question), then a line to create an instance of that record – usually as an array (this is the answer to part **c)**, then code to assign values to the attributes/fields within an instance of the record (the answer shown here in part **d)**.

Question			Answer	Marks available	Commentary, hints and tips
	e)	(i)	Execution error as floating point/real data may be being assigned to an integer variable.	1	Both points are required for the mark to be given. Execution errors are errors that occur while the program is running.
		(ii)	Any two from: ▶ Declare overall as real/single/double/float. ▶ Use a pre-defined function to round the result of the calculation in line 2 to the nearest whole number. ▶ Use a pre-defined function to convert the result of the calculation in line 2 to an integer value.	2	The pre-defined function to convert a real number to an integer is Higher content and this is one way that candidates may be asked about its use.
	f)		Any two from: ▶ There may not be enough storage space to install the app. ▶ There may not be enough main memory to run the app. ▶ The processor may not be fast enough to run the app. ▶ The mobile phone may not be able to run the version of the operating system needed to run the app.	2	An older mobile phone will tend only to be able to update up to a certain version of the operating system. It will also tend to have poorer specification in RAM, processor and storage.
16	a)				
			1 mark for each correct cardinality (1 mark for one Band to many Member, 1 mark for one Band to many Album, 1 mark for one Album to many Song). 1 mark for three correct relationship labels (plays in, releases, contains, or similar). 1 mark for primary keys underlined. 1 mark for asterisks at foreign keys.	6	For two tables to have a relationship, one of the tables must contain a field that is a foreign key. This is the primary key from the other table. Whichever table contains the foreign key is on the 'many' side of a relationship with the table for which that field is the primary key.

Question			Answer	Marks available	Commentary, hints and tips
	b)		1. Y 2. Y 3. Lookup from Album table 1. and 2. for first mark 3. for second mark	2	1. The field indicated is the primary key for the Member table; there must be an entry in this field for every record in that table so that each different member can be uniquely identified. 2. The field indicated is the primary key for the Album table; the entry in this field must be unique for every record in that table so that each different album can be uniquely identified. 3. There can be no entries in this field in the Song table of albums which don't exist in the Album table. A song must appear on an existing album in this database example.
	c)		`SELECT Band.Name, MIN(Peak Chart Position) AS "Best Peak Chart Position" FROM Band, Album, Song WHERE Album.[Band ID] = Band.[Band ID] AND Song.[Album ID] = Album.[Album ID] GROUP BY Band.Name;` 1 mark for `Band.Name` in both `SELECT` and `GROUP BY`. 1 mark for `MIN(Peak Chart Position)`. 1 mark for correct alias `AS "Best Peak Chart Position"`. 1 mark for three correct tables `FROM Band, Album, Song`. 1 mark for two correct equi-joins `WHERE Album.[Band ID] = Band.[Band ID] AND Song.[Album ID] = Album.[Album ID]`.	5	The aggregate function `MIN` finds the smallest value of all the numbers contained in the specified numeric field. An alias is used here to ensure that column of results is headed 'Best Peak Chart Position'. It can be easy to forget the equi-join when the query involves multiple tables so watch out for this. Use of `GROUP BY` here ensures a separate minimum for each band.
	d)		The query will show a list of album names (1 mark) next to the number of songs on that album. (1 mark)	2	The aggregate function `COUNT` counts the number of records returned as the result of the criteria. Use of `GROUP BY` here ensures a separate total for each album rather than the total number of songs in the database.
17	a)	(i)	`<nav>` and `</nav>`	1	These tags ensure the browser knows these links are part of the navigation bar. Hyperlinks can also be used elsewhere in the web page but will only be part of the navigation bar if they appear between these tags.
		(ii)	`<header>` and `</header>`	1	Be careful not to confuse this with the `<head>` tag which appears before the `<body>` section.

Question			Answer	Marks available	Commentary, hints and tips
	b)	(i)	Change line 3 to `<input type="text" name="firstname" size="30" maxlength="25">   `	1	The `maxlength` and `minlength` attributes allow a range check to be applied.
		(ii)	Change line 7 to `<input type="text" name="email" size="60" required>`	1	The required attribute forces an entry in that field before form data can be submitted.
		(iii)	The form's id attribute matches the `<textarea>` form attribute. (1 mark) An (element) id is always unique within a web page. (1 mark)	2	The use of the unique identifier assigned to the form ensures that the browser knows that the text area data is to be submitted as part of the form data.
	c)		`ol li { color:blue; }` (1 mark) `ul li { color:red; }` (1 mark)	2	Descendant selectors allow styling to be applied where the tags mentioned later in the selector are found within the tags mentioned earlier in the selector.
	d)		One from: ▶ change heating based on patterns recognised in stored past usage data ▶ recognise trends in use of certain areas of the building at certain times and turn those zones up or down accordingly ▶ automatically check outside weather and change heating accordingly.	1	Answers must demonstrate in what way the system is intelligent. The best way to answer these types of question is to suggest how the system's programming will allow it to learn from past experience. It will require user input and interaction more often initially but should progress to needing little or no user interaction as long as user behaviour remains the same. It should then respond automatically to data from sensors or other inputs. However, responding to a temperature sensor is not seen as a sign of intelligence as all heating systems do this in some way.
18	a)		Any two from: ▶ Prototypes allow the client to see what the finished product may look like. ▶ The client can clarify/change requirements during development. ▶ A working version of the app can be made available (to customers) more quickly.	2	A problem is initially divided into distinct areas and each area is assigned to a separate development team. It is up to each team to develop their assigned area. They may make extensive use of 'prototyping' to try out ideas rather than following rigid designs. One aim is to produce working code quickly. The clients will be consulted and kept informed throughout the development of a project and give feedback. Careful project management is required to ensure the teams come together at the right times to put the project together.

Question			Answer	Marks available	Commentary, hints and tips
	b)		Any number less than zero – because this is exceptional data that the program should not accept. (1 mark) Zero – because this is extreme data on the boundary of what should be accepted. (1 mark) Either is correct for **X** or **Y**, but one must be extreme and the other exceptional to gain the full 2 marks.	2	The order of your answer isn't important as long as the correct explanation follows each. A good test plan will test normal, extreme and exceptional data. As the table is given in the question, only normal data is present.

	c)		Line 3, one of:
			`SET max TO numberarray[0]`
			`SET max TO 0`
			`DECLARE max INITIALLY 0`
			`DECLARE max INITIALLY numberarray[0]`
			Lines 7, 8, 9:
			`IF number > max THEN`
			`    SET max TO number`
			`END IF`
			1 mark for line 3 and line 8 correct.
			1 mark for line 7 and line 9 correct.
				2	This is a version of the 'find the maximum' standard algorithm. Variations in the language/wording of your answer from the answer given here will be accepted, as long as the meaning is the same as that given here. Forgetting to end the IF is a frequent mistake.

19	a)		`SET total to 0`
			`FOR EACH entry FROM age DO`
			`        IF age < 18 THEN`
			`                SET total TO total+1`
			`        END IF`
			`END FOR`
			`SEND total TO DISPLAY`
			1 mark for intialising total to 0.
			1 mark for correct loop/end loop.
			1 mark for `IF` with correct condition and `END IF`.
			1 mark for increment total.
			1 mark for displaying total.
				5	This is an example of the 'count occurrences' standard algorithm. The first line could also be `DECLARE total INITIALLY 0`.

	b)		Dunton Juniors should obtain a digital certificate for their site (1 mark) as this is authenticated/issued by a certification authority. (1 mark) OR as this means the site is regulated. (1 mark)	2	Digital certificates are issued by a third party that confirms the identity of a website. The certificate contains the name of the certificate holder, a serial number, expiration dates, a copy of the certificate holder's public key and the digital signature of the certificate-issuing authority.

Question			Answer	Marks available	Commentary, hints and tips
	c)		The data is encrypted on the user's device using Dunton Juniors' public key (1 mark) and the data is decrypted at the destination using Dunton Juniors' private key. (1 mark)	2	This form of encryption involves two algorithms for encryption/decryption. If you encrypt using one, you can decrypt using the other, and vice versa. One algorithm is therefore released to the public as the public key – users can encrypt using this algorithm. The second algorithm which could decrypt the data is kept secret – as a private key. So only the one who released the public key can decrypt data encrypted by that public key – it is decrypted through the use of the private key.

	d)		`p, footer, header, img, main: { padding: 9px; }`
			
			`p, img: { margin-top:4px; margin-bottom: 4px; }`
			
			`footer, header: { margin-top:8px; margin-bottom: 5px; }`
			
			`main: { margin-top:6px; margin-bottom: 6px; }`
			
			1 mark for each correct rule above.
				4	Grouping selectors allow the same rule to be applied to multiple elements quickly and easily for the person creating the web page.

	e)		Any two from: ▸ access the home page, to see if images are displayed as expected ▸ check the validation on the form to log in to the site ▸ check the validation on the form to pay for a season ticket.	2	Testing of websites at Higher level involves not only usability and compatibility testing, but also input validation, i.e. that any navigational bar works and that media content displays correctly.
20	a)		 1 mark for correct first level. 1 mark for correct second level.	2	Larger websites could contain hundreds or even thousands of web pages. If these are organised into a clear structure with levels and sub-levels it is much easier for users to browse. They can then find the page they are looking for without passing through many irrelevant pages or trying to use a search facility which may omit the page they want if the search terms are not worded in the particular way that they appear within the desired page. A hierarchical structure (with multilevel navigation) aids usability.
	b)		`img {float: left; }`	1	This tells the images to appear at the left of their section on the web page, next to other elements in that section.

Question			Answer	Marks available	Commentary, hints and tips
	c)		`.locations {clear: both; }` 1 mark for `.locations` 1 mark for `clear: both`	2	Here a class is used to ensure the rule only applies to elements assigned to that class (locations). This rule states that both sides of the element must be kept clear – another element cannot appear next to this one.
	d)		Photographs do not have distinct/separate shapes which are required for vector storage. OR Vector storage does not allow for individually coloured pixels which are required to represent a photograph.	1	Vector graphics are stored using text to represent objects and attributes, whereas bitmap files are stored using a binary colour code for each pixel.
21	a)		The possibility of clashes between variable names. (1 mark) It may be difficult for multiple programmers to work on the code. (1 mark)	2	Code would be less readable/harder to maintain (as the flow of data is less clear). Note that in the past SQA also accepted that code cannot be easily re-used or code is less portable/modular. SQA also accepted in the past that global variables have a greater impact or load on main memory. However, neither of these appeared in the marking scheme for the recent specimen paper for a similar question.
	b)		Functions return a value. (1 mark) Procedures perform a list of commands OR procedures may change multiple variables OR procedures may not change any variables OR procedures change variables through parameters. (1 mark)	2	Functions can be pre-defined (included by the creators of the programming language) or user-defined (created by a programmer using the language – NOT a user). Variables passed into a function are 'arguments'. Functions are called using `SET`; for example, to call the `LEN` function: `SET length TO LEN(name)` The `name` variable is the argument in this example.
	c)		Vector graphics have a smaller file size. (1 mark) Second mark, any of: ▶ will take less time to download ▶ will use up less data allowance if downloaded over 3G/4G ▶ will require less main memory/RAM in mobile device ▶ will require less storage on mobile device.	2	Vector graphics are stored using text to represent objects and attributes, whereas bitmap files are stored using a binary colour code for each pixel.

Question			Answer	Marks available	Commentary, hints and tips

	d)		Set max to -1
			Set maxposition to -1
			Loop for each venue
			  If current price <= target cost and current
			  capacity > max then
			    max = current capacity
			    maxposition = current position
			  End if
			End for loop
			Return maxposition
			1 mark for initial set of max and maxposition.
			1 mark for using the condition current price <= target cost.
			1 mark for using the condition current capacity > max.
			1 mark for setting new max.
			1 mark for setting new maxposition.
				5	You are advised to answer questions of this type using pseudocode; however, it is acceptable to answer using a structure diagram or flowchart. Where the algorithm involves a condition in order for a result to be acceptable, you can't set the first item in the array to be the initial maximum as it may not meet the condition. Here the condition is that the cost of the venue is less than the cost entered by the user.

22	a)		 1 mark 1 mark		
				2	An entity-occurrence diagram shows data within each entity – effectively showing the relationship between individual records. As such it is a snapshot of the state of a database at a particular (often theoretical) time. Data within most databases will frequently change so an entity-occurrence diagram will only reflect the actual state of a database if no edits have yet been made to the data since the diagram was created.

Question		Answer	Marks available	Commentary, hints and tips
	b)	SELECT [Event Name] (1 mark) FROM Event, Charity (1 mark) WHERE Charity.Location LIKE "*Ayrshire" (1 mark) AND Event.[Charity ID] = Charity.[Charity ID]; (1 mark)	4	Some applications use '*' as the wildcard character and some use '%'. Either are acceptable, so it is correct to have SELECT [Event Name] FROM Event, Charity WHERE Charity.Location LIKE "%Ayrshire" AND Event.[Charity ID] = Charity.[Charity ID];
	c)	Tables: Staff, Event, Charity (1 mark) Fields: Staff.Forename, Staff.Surname, Event.Event Name, Event.Location, Charity.Charity Name (1 mark) Criteria: Staff ID = S001 (1 mark)	3	Questions in this format have been included in Higher papers in the past. The logic is the same as when you construct SQL SELECT queries, so try not to be put off by structuring your answer a little differently.
	d)	COUNT( ) or COUNT([Event ID])	1	The aggregate function COUNT counts the number of records returned as the result of the criteria.

Practice Paper 2
Section 1

Question			Answer	Marks available	Commentary, hints and tips
1			−2048 to +2047 OR −2^{12−1} to (2^{12−1})−1 1 mark for upper limit. 1 mark for lower limit.	2	Two's complement allows storage of both positive and negative numbers. The total number of possible numbers that can be stored with 12 bits is 2^{12} which is 4096 possible numbers. With two's complement, half of those possible numbers will be negative, so the lower limit is −2048. One of the possible numbers is zero. So, there are only 2047 possible positive integers. This means the upper limit is 2047.
2			Earlier stages are revisited (1 mark) after new information has been gained at a later stage in the process. (1 mark)	2	The term 'iterative' means that a process repeats. While it can be tempting to explain the iterative nature of this software development methodology by using an example, any example must include the key points given here. One example of this could be that a logic error is found at the testing stage, therefore the earlier design stage and implementation stage are revisited in order to correct the error due to the information gained from the testing stage.
3			<table><tr><td>sign</td><td>0</td></tr><tr><td>mantissa</td><td>110 0001 1000 0000</td></tr><tr><td>exponent</td><td>00000011</td></tr></table> 1 mark for correct sign bit. 1 mark for correct 15 bits for mantissa. 1 mark for correct 8 bits for exponent.	3	$110.00011 = 0.11000011 \times 2^3$ The sign bit is 0 if the number is positive, and 1 if the number is negative. The sign bit counts as one of the 16 bits assigned to the mantissa. Any 'extra' unneeded bits in the mantissa are set to zero and appear at the far right of the number – away from the side where the decimal point has moved to (or else they would be 'significant' and affect the value of the number). If the exponent is negative then it is stored using two's complement.

Question			Answer	Marks available	Commentary, hints and tips
4			Any two from: ▶ cache stores frequently/recently accessed instructions/data ▶ variables used more than once in the algorithm will be present in cache (examples acceptable) ▶ later instructions in the algorithm could be pre-loaded into cache (no branches/IFs to affect this).	2	Cache memory is a small amount of static RAM placed on the same chip as the processor. Take care not to say 'closer to the processor' as a reason for using cache as this is not accepted. Cache will store the contents of any recently accessed memory locations but will also 'look ahead' and pre-fetch what should be the next instruction in the sequence as a program executes. This feature is only of use, however, if the program does not branch due to a condition and requires a different instruction to be fetched.
5			The statement is not fit for purpose (1 mark) as it will delete all the records from the Volunteer table (1 mark) but leave the table with its fields present in the database. (1 mark)	3	DELETE is only used to delete records and not tables.
6			`<link rel = "stylesheet" type= "text/css" href= "webstyle.css">` 1 mark for link. 1 mark for type.	2	This must be placed in the head section of the HTML to apply the styling contained within the external stylesheet to the web page. Be careful to include '.css' at the end of the file name.
7	a)		`RECORD songdetails IS {STRING title, STRING artist, INTEGER highest chart position}` 1 mark for an obvious record structure with a name. 1 mark for all fields with correct data types.	2	A record allows a set of variables, with different types, to be named and organised under one data structure. This answer defines that a record called songdetails exists, but no instances of the record have been created yet. All text in capitals in the answer here is required exactly as shown. The names (in lower case) were not stated in the question, so just have to be sensible.

	b)		`DIM songCollection[4999] as songdetails`
			OR
			`DECLARE songCollection AS ARRAY OF songdetails INITIALLY [ ] * 4999`
			OR
			`Create variable songCollection[4999] of data type songdetails`
			1 mark for array with value.
			1 mark for data type from record created in part a).
				2	As you can see from the answer choices given, the ideas are more important than the strict syntax of the answer. Be sure to use whichever name you used in your answer to a) as a data type for a variable/array with a new name not seen yet in your paper. In this example, the variable/array has been named songCollection. Be sure to indicate the array size in square brackets.

Question			Answer	Marks available	Commentary, hints and tips
8	a)		The range of code statements for which a variable is valid.	1	The scope of a global variable is the whole program. The scope of a local variable is the subprogram it is created in – unless the variable is passed into other subprograms using parameter passing.
	b)		Any one from: ▶ parameter passing ▶ pass by value or reference ▶ declare as local or global.	1	
9			Change the first line shown to `<select name="flavour" size="5" multiple>` 1 mark for `size="5"`. 1 mark for `multiple`.	2	The drop-down menu allows you to limit the possible choices. The size attribute determines how many options are visible at one time, and multiple allows for more than one option to be selected. Radio buttons are not suitable here as they do not allow multiple selections to be made at the same time.
10			When the page loads the image in the file official.jpg is shown. (1 mark) When the pointer is over the image, the file celebrate.jpg is shown. (1 mark) When the pointer leaves the image, the file official.jpg is shown. (1 mark)	3	This is often known as a rollover image. The JavaScript is used to change an attribute of the image when the mouse is moved over and restore the attribute to its original value when the mouse is moved off again.

Section 2

Question			Answer	Marks available	Commentary, hints and tips
| 11 | a) | | ```
SET found TO false
FOR index FROM 0 TO 7 DO
   IF name(index) = target_name THEN
      SET found TO true
      SET target_sold TO sold(index)
   END IF
END FOR
IF found THEN
   SEND "The... of" & target_name &
"was" &
   target_sold TO DISPLAY
ELSE
   SEND "That type is not in the
list" TO DISPLAY
END IF
``` 1 mark for two correct settings of Boolean. (line 1, line 4) <br> 1 mark for use of correct fixed loop, with end loop. <br> 1 mark for first `IF` statement with the correct condition and `END IF`. <br> 1 mark for assigning a variable to `sold(index)` within the first `IF`. <br> 1 mark for second `IF` statement with the correct condition and `END IF`. <br> 1 mark for outputs to screen (both `SEND... TO DISPLAY`). | 6 | This is a version of the 'linear search' standard algorithm. <br><br> Other structures of this solution are possible. |
	b)	(i)	49	1	A trace table is a paper and pencil exercise following a set of data through a program and noting how each variable changes at different points in the program. If the value of a variable is different from the expected value, an error has occurred.
		(ii)	65	1	
	c)		The program tries to access an array element that does not exist (array out of bounds execution error). (1 mark) Use a variable/parameter to store the size of the array. OR Change the number 7 to `END OF LIST`. OR Use a function to get the size of the array. OR Use a conditional loop and loop until end of list. OR Change 7 to 6 (line 2). (1 mark)	2	It is good programming practice to avoid numeric constants in your program where possible. Declaring these as variables instead at the beginning of your program means that, should a change be necessary, only one change needs to be made. However, in this situation, there are several solutions that give the desired flexibility, as shown. An execution error is one that occurs while the program is running.
```

Question			Answer	Marks available	Commentary, hints and tips
	d)	(i)	Count occurrences	1	

		(ii)	`SET total TO 0`
			`FOR index FROM 0 TO 6 DO`
			`  IF sold(index)>= 30 THEN`
			`    SET total TO total + 1`
			`  END IF`
			`END FOR`
			`SEND total & " types sold 30 or more" TO DISPLAY`
			
			1 mark for initialising total to zero and adding one to the total within the `IF`.
			1 mark for correct `FOR` and `NEXT`.
			1 mark for correct `IF` and `END IF`.
			1 mark for showing result on screen.
				4	This algorithm will use a fixed loop to traverse the array and keep a running total of entries that meet the condition.

	e)		Any two of: ▸ name of function ▸ name of argument(s) ▸ data type of argument(s) ▸ return data type.	2	An argument is a piece of data passed into a function that is required for the code within the function to perform the task it was designed to perform. A function always returns one value to the calling program/ subprogram.
12	a)		Category to Product is one-to-many. Manufacturer to Product is one-to-many. Exporter to Manufacturer is one-to-many. (1 mark each)	3	For two tables to have a relationship, one of the tables must contain a field which is a foreign key; that is the primary key from the other table. Whichever table contains the foreign key is on the 'many' side of a relationship with the table for which that field is the primary key.
	b)		2 marks for five correct fields or 1 mark for four correct fields. 1 mark for three correct tables. 1 mark for correct search criteria.	4	Take care to use the field names as given in the description of the database, not those that appear on the screenshot of the web page, as those labels are often different. For the search criteria, `Product.ProductID` is the only entry shown on the query result that is guaranteed to be unique – the shop may sell 'soor plooms' from a number of different manufacturers, so the product name is not an appropriate answer here.

Field(s) and calculation(s)	Product.Name Product.Product ID Product.Description Manufacturer.Name Category.Current Discount
Table(s) and query	Product, Manufacturer, Category
Search criteria	`Product.Product ID=0042`
Grouping	
Sort order	

Question			Answer	Marks available	Commentary, hints and tips

	c)		```
			<script>
			function mouseOver() {
			document.getElementById("dani").
			style.color = "blue";
			}
			</script>
			``
			1 mark for opening and closing script tags.
			1 mark for function mouseOver
			1 mark for document.getElementById("dani")
			1 mark for.style.color = "blue"
				4	The HTML h1 element in the question has already been given the id dani, so be sure to use this. The inclusion of onmouseover="mouseOver()" ensures that the mouseOver() function will be called when the pointer moves over the relevant text – your answer need only show what happens within that function. Be sure to spell 'color' in the US way.
					
					In practice it is possible to call the mouseover function and send in the calling element as a parameter.

13	a)		left OR back (1 mark) An actual parameter is a variable in use in the program that calls the subprogram/function/procedure. OR A copy of an actual parameter can be created and sent to a subprogram/function/procedure. OR A pointer to the actual parameter can be sent to a subprogram/function/procedure. (1 mark)	2	The actual parameters are created within the part of the program that then goes on to call the subprogram or function. These variables can be passed into the subprogram by value or by reference. If an actual parameter is passed in by value, the formal parameter will be a copy of the actual parameter, which will only exist for the life of the subprogram and will have no effect on the original variable (that is, the actual parameter). If an actual parameter is passed by reference then the formal parameter will contain a pointer to the actual parameter and any change made to the formal parameter will in fact change the actual parameter. Passing by value or reference allows the programmer to control the flow of data.
	b)	(i)	8	1	
		(ii)	Change line 7 to ELSE IF hours_hired <=2 THEN	1	The second IF is wrongly placed inside the first IF, so if the hours_hired is not less than 1, the second IF is never tested. However if hours_hired is less than 1, the second IF ensures that the higher charge of eight overwrites the lower charge of 5.

Question			Answer	Marks available	Commentary, hints and tips
	c)		Execution of the program will pause at a specified line of code. (1 mark) The programmer can compare values of variables with expected values. (1 mark)	2	There are two ways to pause the program mid-execution in order to check if the variables contain the data the tester believes they should. Breakpoints are set on a specific line of code, so the program will pause when that line has been executed. Watchpoints are set on a particular variable, so that the program can be set to pause either whenever that variable is accessed or whenever that variable is changed.
	d)		`hours_hired` within the function is a local variable.	1	A local variable is one which is not passed as a parameter and is instead only valid in the subprogram it appears within. Use of local variables allows variables of the same name in different modules without affecting others. Also using local variables makes a program more modular, as parts can be developed in isolation by different programmers, or more easily transferred between programs with little or no change. Local variables are more efficient, as memory assigned to a local variable becomes available once the function is ended.
	e)		IN: `profit[]` (1 mark) OUT: `total` (1 mark)	2	The dates are not required when counting the number of entries in the `profit[]` array that meet the criteria. In data flow, if a step changes a variable then that variable is said to flow OUT of the step. If the step uses a variable then that variable is said to flow IN to the step.
| | f) | | ```
FOR i FROM 0 TO 364 DO
   SET date[i] TO date[i]
(0:5)&"20"&date[i](6:7)
NEXT i
``` 1 mark for fixed loop and end loop. 1 mark for two correct substrings. 1 mark for assignment and concatenation. | 3 | Each language does substring differently but whichever way you use in class will be accepted if correct. |
```

Question			Answer	Marks available	Commentary, hints and tips
14	a)		Any two from: ▶ test with a specific user group/novice/expert ▶ can assign tasks to test certain areas of the site ▶ can receive feedback to improve the user's experience.	2	Usability testing is a way to see how easy a program or website is to use by testing it with real users. They are asked to complete set tasks while they are being observed by a researcher to see where they encounter problems. The observed results are fed back to the development team to improve the final version.
	b)	(i)	The colour (code) of the affected/relevant pixels would be changed. (Pixels where the oval has moved from are changed from black to white, pixels where the oval has moved to are changed from white to black.)	1	Vector graphics are stored as text. The text is the list of objects (shapes) and their attributes. Attributes include line colour, fill colour, coordinates and the layer the shape is on. Adding a new object adds more text to the file, so increases file size. The system uses the text to produce the image, it is not stored at a set resolution, so the resolution is determined by the available hardware – scaling will not lead to pixelation. This is known as resolution independence. Bitmapped graphics are stored using a colour code for each pixel in the image. To move or remove an object involves changing the colour code for the relevant pixels. These images are saved at a set resolution when created.
		(ii)	Attributes/coordinates of the shape will be changed (can be done by dragging the shape or editing the text of the file).	1	
	c)	(i)	New designs have a higher file size (1 mark) as new shapes/instructions/attributes have been added. (1 mark)	2	
		(ii)	No change to file size (1 mark) as the colour of existing pixels has been changed but no new pixels have been added. (1 mark)	2	

Question			Answer	Marks available	Commentary, hints and tips

15	a)		OPEN FILE "stats.txt"
			FOR counter FROM 0 TO 31 DO
			    RECEIVE authority(counter).name FROM FILE
			    RECEIVE authority(counter).annual_rainfall FROM
			    FILE
			    RECEIVE authority(counter).hours_sunshine
			    FROM FILE
			    RECEIVE authority(counter).average_windspeed
			    FROM FILE
			END FOR
			CLOSE FILE
			1 mark for open and close file.
			1 mark for correct fixed loop/end loop.
			1 mark for correct relation of field name to record name.
			1 mark for reading from file using counter correctly to index the array.
				4	Remember, arrays are indexed from zero. Dot notation is often used when referencing attributes of records within programs. However, if you just have
					`authority.name`
					the program wouldn't know which of the authorities you are referring to, so the correct syntax is either
					`authority(counter).name`
					or
					`authority.name(counter).`

	b)		Any two from: ▸ Jiong's windspeeds are of type real, this function processes windspeeds of type integer. ▸ This function returns only the number of the highest windspeed, not the name of the authority this corresponds to. ▸ Jiong's windspeeds are attributes within an array of records, he cannot pass only the windspeeds as an array into this function as an argument.	2	The arguments are the parameters passed into a function so that it can do its job. Rebekah's function here expects one argument, an array of integers. Jiong has used an array of records, so the function would have to be changed to accept an array of records. Once this had been done, it could then be further changed to find the name of the authority with the highest average windspeed.

Question			Answer	Marks available	Commentary, hints and tips
16	a)			5	For two tables to have a relationship, one of the tables must contain a field which is a foreign key that is the primary key from the other table. Whichever table contains the foreign key is on the 'many' side of a relationship with the table for which that field is the primary key.
			1 mark for each correct cardinality (one Venue to many Instructor, one Venue to many Booking, one Venue to many Track). 1 mark for three correct relationship labels (works in, is for, contains, or similar). 1 mark for primary keys underlined and asterisks at foreign keys.		
	b)		Specific processes/instructions/tasks/bikes can be allocated to certain processors/cores (1 mark) allowing concurrent/simultaneous execution/parallel processing. (1 mark)	2	Multicore processors allow parallel processing: multiple processes being serviced simultaneously. With a number of bikes sending simultaneous updates, this is clearly advantageous in this situation.
	c)		`UPDATE Booking` (1 mark) `SET [No. Riders]=[No.Riders]+2` (1 mark) `WHERE [Booking ID]=0361;` (1 mark)	3	An update query is used to change the values contained in a field. Usually this is combined with criteria so that only some records are changed, and some are not.

Question			Answer	Marks available	Commentary, hints and tips
	d)		SELECT Venue.Name, SUM(Booking.[No. Riders]) AS "Total Riders" FROM Booking, Venue WHERE Booking.Date>31/12/2017 AND Booking.Date<1/1/2019 AND Booking.[Venue Postcode] = Venue.[Venue Postcode] GROUP BY Venue.Name 1 mark for Venue.Name in both SELECT and GROUP BY. 1 mark for SUM(Booking.[No. Riders]). 1 mark for alias AS "Total Riders". 1 mark for FROM Booking, Venue. 1 mark for correct dates Booking.Date>31/12/2017 AND Booking.Date<1/1/2019 inside WHERE clause. 1 mark for equi-join Booking.[Venue Postcode] = Venue.[Venue Postcode] inside WHERE clause.	6	The aggregate function SUM adds up the values of all the numbers contained in the specified numeric field. An alias is used here to ensure that the column of results is headed 'Total Riders'. It can be easy to forget the equi-join when the query involves multiple tables so watch out for this. Use of GROUP BY here ensures a separate total for each venue, rather than the overall total of visitors the company has had that year.
17	a)		Any two from: ▶ store/display images/artwork ▶ allow user/artist to log in ▶ allow user payment/sign up ▶ allow artist upload of images/artwork.	2	Functional requirements are tasks that the website must be able to perform. User requirements are tasks that users of the website must be able to perform. Any answers that begin 'users must be able to…' are considered to be user requirements and will not be given marks when you are asked for functional requirements.
	b)		Any two from: ▶ button to submit login data ▶ link to sign-up page in case user does not yet have an account ▶ link back to free section in case user does not wish to sign up ▶ header section/navigation bar to ensure consistency/usability ▶ footer section to ensure consistency.	2	The user interface would be more user-friendly if a 'Submit' button was present. Navigation bars also aid usability as a user can see how to quickly and easily access multiple parts of the site – which will often be arranged by category and in a multilevel structure.

Question			Answer	Marks available	Commentary, hints and tips
	c)	(i)	170 pixels	1	The CSS rule shown applies only to the first image as the second img tag is not within a p tag. The first image will have below it 70 pixels of padding and 100 pixels of margin before the second image begins.
		(ii)	Any four from: ▶ no change to comicstrip1.jpg/the first image ▶ as the same CSS formatting/rules are applied ▶ CSS formatting/rules now apply to comicstrip2.jpg/the second image ▶ so this image will now be shown 85 pixels from the left ▶ the gap between the two images will now be 290 pixels.	4	Margins determine the space between different elements, padding determines the space between the border of the element and the content contained within the element. Search the web for 'CSS Box Model' to see a visual representation of this.

	d)		```html
			<footer>
			Comic strips per page:
			
			<form>
			<select>
			<option value="1">1</option>
			<option value="2">2</option>
			<option value="3">3</option>
			<option value="4">4</option>
			<option value="5">5</option>
			</select>
			<input type="submit" value="Submit">
			</form>
			</footer>
			``
			1 mark for <footer> and </footer>.
			1 mark for <form> and </form>.
			1 mark for <select> and </select>.
			1 mark for five correct options.
			1 mark for submit button.
				5	The footer tag is used for HTML code that will appear at the bottom of multiple pages.
					It is also acceptable to answer with a number input instead of a drop-down menu:
					``html
					<footer>
					Comic strips per page:
					
					<form>
					<input type="number" min="1" max="5">
					<input type="submit" value="Submit">
					</form>
					</footer>
					``
					In this case the third mark would be for <input type="number">
					and the fourth mark would be for min="1" max="5"

	e)		Any of: ▶ user/functional requirements in order to evaluate fitness for purpose ▶ results of testing in order to evaluate fitness for purpose ▶ feedback/results of usability testing in order to evaluate usability.	1	

Notes

Notes